Off the Charts

OFF THE CHARTS

What I Learned From My Almost Fabulous Life in Music

KAT GOLDMAN

sh.

SUTHERLAND HOUSE

TORONTO, 2021

Sutherland House
416 Moore Ave., Suite 205
Toronto, ON M4G 1C9

First edition, September 2020

If you are interested in inviting one of our authors to a live event or
media appearance, please contact publicity@sutherlandhousebooks.com
and visit our website at sutherlandhousebooks.com for more
information about our authors and their schedules.

Manufactured in the United States
Cover designed by Lena Yang
Book composed by Karl Hunt

Library and Archives Canada Cataloguing in Publication
Title: Off the charts : what I learned from my
almost fabulous life in music / Kat Goldman.
Names: Goldman, Kat, 1970- author.
Identifiers: Canadiana 20200267981 | ISBN 9781989555323 (hardcover)
Subjects: LCSH: Goldman, Kat, 1970- | LCSH: Singers—Canada—Biography. |
LCSH: Composers—Canada—
Biography. | LCGFT: Autobiographies.
Classification: LCC ML420.G619 A3 2020 |
DDC 782.42164092—dc23

ISBN 978-1-989555-32-3

THIS BOOK IS DEDICATED TO
MY PARENTS

Foreword

A COUPLE OF YEARS AGO, I received an email from a folk music disc jockey well-known in the New York scene. We were discussing Kat Goldman's new album *The Workingman's Blues*. The disc jockey said she could not understand why Kat was not more famous. I, too, pondered this question.

I had been a fan since I first heard her song "Annabel," about the passing of her grandmother. I was blown away by the lyrics and the angelic voice. The song was later recorded by the Winnipeg-based band the Duhks, but to me there is no comparison to the melody, lyrics, and vocal work of Kat's original version. It brings tears to the eyes of listeners.

Enthralled by Kat's creativity, I probed our question further and began acquiring more of her catalogue. I learned that the evolution of Kat Goldman has not been a straight line. Two weeks prior to moving to Brooklyn in 2007, and before the release of her second album, *Sing Your Song*, she was involved in a freak accident that essentially put her career on hiatus. She endured a long and difficult recovery, and never made it to New York, which had been her lifelong dream.

After a long recovery from the accident, and bouts of depression, Kat moved to Boston to attend school, earning a degree in English literature at Boston University. She was also able to record the album *Gypsy Girl*.

A failing relationship and the need to return home to Canada prompted the production of the album *The Workingman's Blues*, which is about the loves, lives, and struggles of the working class in America. I interviewed Kat for my podcast, *Mostly Folk*, and was blown away all over again by her story, her voice, and her lyrics.

Much later, I was listening to "Weight of the World" on Dar Williams's 2015 album, *Emerald*. I've had some hearing loss that can affect my full comprehension and I wanted to make sure I understood the lyrics, so I checked the lyric sheet. I was thinking that Dar had done it again, writing another incredibly moving song. Then I saw the song was written by Kat. I was floored. How had I missed such a wonderful song?

And now she's written a book. Kat calls it a how-to guide for the beginning songwriter and, indeed, it should be read by everyone trying to climb the ladder to fame in the music industry, or in any industry where you have to stand on a stage in front of an audience. Musicians, comedians, magicians, and clowns will all learn something from this book. Kat's experiences and reminiscences are priceless. If I were starting out as a performer, I'd want to know everything she knows.

But the book is so much more. It is packed with hysterical personal stories that will make performers and fans alike laugh out loud. Every chapter is heartfelt and delightful, brimming with insight and wisdom. As you share her journey, consider yourself one of the fortunate.

Artie Martello
DJ/Producer
Mostly Folk Podcast
Power Folk on Blues and Roots Radio
The Catskills Café on WIOX 91.3 FM
Halcottsville, New York

The Songwriter as Outsider

HAVE YOU EVER FELT DIFFERENT, weird, or like you don't belong? Do you tend to think outside the box? Would you be described as a square peg in a round hole? Are you shy and quiet, a loner in your life? Were you ever teased or bullied as a child? It could be because you're a songwriter.

Were you the person in high school who sat in the corner at parties, strumming your guitar? Did you stay up long nights in manic bursts of writing? Did you find you had to write song lyrics on a small pad of paper when you were in the middle of some other activity, like doing downward dog in yoga class, or playing tennis with a friend? It could be you're a songwriter.

Are you prone to mood swings? Do you have trouble concentrating? Would your friends describe you as a bit absent-minded? I know a guy who walked thirty minutes in a snowstorm in his long johns before he realized he wasn't wearing any pants. He's one of the best songwriters I know.

What I'm trying to say is that the songwriter might always feel like the odd person out. But you know what? It's okay to be different. Writing and singing songs is your superpower. Don't forget this on days when you're feeling down. We need to celebrate our gifts and embrace our own unique natures.

And you are not alone. There are so many other songwriters out there. It's become trendy, like wearing Lacoste T-shirts was in the eighties. But all those songwriters are your kindred spirits. We are all in this together.

Checking One, Two, Three . . .

OFTEN, DURING THEIR SOUND CHECKS, performers will say into the microphone: "Checking one, two, three."

A really experienced performer will say: "Checking one, two, two, *tewwww* . . ." and they will let the "ewwww" ring out for a bit, as if trying to make sense of the sound they are hearing.

Sometimes they will make a clucking sound, like when you pop your tongue off the roof of your mouth.

Or else they will say: "Check, check, check," but they will say it so fast it sounds like: "Chk-chk-chk."

These are things that can't be taught, but that you learn by *doing*, as a songwriter.

What I do is a combination of approaches. I will say: "Checking one, two, *two*, two—three, two, four . . . *tewwwwwww*," and then I will make a couple of the clucking sounds off the roof of my mouth.

Then I will go back to the beginning and say: "Checking one . . . two . . . three . . . four . . . a-five, a-six, a-five, six, seven, eight!"

And then I will kick my right leg into the air, and then my left, and I will start to shake out my arms to get the circulation going, making full circles around my body, followed by a couple of jumping jacks, all the while making the clucking sounds into the microphone.

The sound person sometimes looks a bit flustered when I do this, and he or she might begin to roll his or her eyes from behind the soundboard. Do not let this deter you from the task at hand. It's *your* show and you need to do whatever it is to make yourself comfortable during your sound check.

Now, just because your soundperson is dressed in black with all kinds of tattoos on his arms and the back of his neck, piercings in his eyebrows, and has a heavy metal chain hanging from his pocket does not mean you should be intimidated by him.

Just because he will be the *sole* person responsible for making your sound good that night does not mean you should kowtow to him, or bat your eyelashes and pretend you don't know anything about music: "Ohhh, was I supposed to plug my patch cord into the input? Tee hee!"

By the same token, you don't have to try to impress your soundperson, saying: "Can I have some more bass on my guitar?" Even though you have no idea what that means but you think it sounds good.

Whatever you do, don't piss off your soundperson, acting all cocky and rock star–ish when you get onstage. Remember, they will have *their* hands on the dials during your show.

Instead, try to approach your sound person like your equal, like you are in this together. Maybe he (or she), too, collects comic books, or enjoys Thai food. When you get to the gig, you might want to say, "Hey," slap them on the back, and make a point of connecting. And then take your time.

Don't let anyone—a manager, headliner, or soundperson—make you rush your sound check. Do what you need to feel grounded in your show. Get things just as you like them: maybe a little reverb, or more sound in your vocal monitor.

There used to be a rumour around New York City that if you tipped your soundperson, he or she would make your sound extra-good. I am gullible, so I handed a $20-bill to the sound guy at the Bitter End. He seemed pretty happy about it, albeit a tad confused.

Don't offer your money to the soundperson. You can't afford it! But maybe you can offer one of your CDs. Who knows? You might even make a new fan out of him. And maybe you will make a new friend.

Advice on Dating Rock Stars

TAKE MY ADVICE. *Never* date a rock star. They can be *so* selfish! When you wake up in the morning, a rock star will not make you a coffee, even though he will already be sipping one himself.

"Oh. Did you want a coffee?" he will say, acting surprised.

"It's good to be on the road," and then he will throw you and your baggage to the curb.

"Rock on!" he will say, making the rock 'n' roll sign with his knuckles and two fingers as you drive away, perplexed.

He will kick you out of his loft so fast you won't have a chance to eat breakfast. Not even a bowl of muesli. It will leave you famished. Rock stars can be so uncaring. They almost never make for good boyfriends.

Also, it's true what they say, that their guitars are really just an extension of their sex organs. Why else would they go on and on, "shredding it" in their solos? The only reason they ever picked up their instrument in the first place was to get the girls! Yet anytime you want to have some meaningful kind of conversation with them, they will start to play the guitar solo from "Hotel California."

And don't be deceived by their good looks! Just an excuse for bad behavior and an endless trail of promiscuity! How will you ever know whether to believe them when they tell you the women they write about in their songs are "fictional"? You will always wonder if they're grabbing someone else's fanny on the road.

One time I got into his passenger seat, and a rock star yelled at me for slamming his car door too hard. (They can be so temperamental!) I wondered how you shut the car door softly—without making any noise—and still effectively close it. Not only that, you have to constantly stroke their egos and tell them they're great, or else rock stars will go ballistic and begin to throw things in the air such as their cell phone chargers.

Also, rock stars have very short attention spans. They will completely ignore you unless you are wearing a cool yellow vintage sweater dress. This will captivate them for a while, until some hotter woman walks through the door, and suddenly you are chopped liver. In general, they only take notice of you for about fifteen minutes. Beyond that, their eyes begin to glaze over.

I'm telling you. Never date a rock star. They're the worst!

Busking

RECENTLY WATCHED A CLIP of Alanis Morissette busking in the New York subway. When people started to recognize it was her, a huge crowd gathered around. They were singing along to "You Oughta Know," clapping and cheering in sheer delight. Well, all I can say is, that wasn't *my* experience of busking.

Try standing outside for hours on end, your fingers so cold it hurts to strum your guitar! Try singing over the noise of honking trucks and ambulance sirens with dust and garbage whipping in your face! I was shifting from leg to leg because I had to go to the bathroom. My nose was running and I had no free hand to wipe it. I blew out my vocal cords because I didn't have a sound system. And for what? The measly few dollars people threw into my guitar case?

Some performers busk for the fun of it, I guess. But I would just like to know, are they nuts? Busking is the bottom of the venue barrel. It's for when you literally can't find a dive bar that will have you play.

I'm told there are some people who can make money at it but mostly it depends on what city you're busking in. One time I was playing at the corner of Bloor and Spadina in Toronto and an elderly couple gave me a loaf of bread.

"Are you *okay*?" they asked me, leaning in close. "Do you have a place to stay tonight?"

That was unsettling but better than the look of horror on the faces of friends, colleagues, relatives, and ex-boyfriends when they see you standing on a street corner with a guitar strapped around your neck.

Busking in Toronto is pretty much frowned upon. It doesn't help that you have to audition to get a licence to do it. I think it's sad we don't have a culture in Toronto that supports the open and free expression of creativity in outdoor spaces.

Busking in Boston was different. It got you more acclaim. It was even cool when I lived there in the nineties. Buskers had to get to Harvard Square early in the morning to claim their spot because there was so much competition. Often you could see great talents. Many went on to have respectable songwriting careers, like Martin Sexton, Tracy Chapman, and a duo called the Story. I once watched the Story set up two microphones in Harvard Square and within minutes they had a huge crowd sitting around them on the sidewalk.

Busking in certain countries in Europe was also profitable around that time. In 1993, my friend Esther and I performed Simon and Garfunkel covers at a café in a train station in Paris. We went around to every table with a colourful Guatemalan cap to collect money and made close to $70. It was just enough to buy our train tickets to Prague. It was fun. Then again it was summer, so there were no frostbitten fingers.

The only good things I can see coming from busking are that you get to practise your material and strengthen your singing voice for when you do go into the studio or play shows indoors, with a sound system. And you never know, you might meet some interesting people while you're at it. Like the guy who was doing pirouettes beside me all day in Harvard Square in his bare feet and army fatigues. (At least it was company!)

Fans

WHEN FOR THE FIRST TIME somebody asks you for your autograph, your initial response might be to chuckle. The first few times I was asked for my autograph, I giggled to myself for several minutes. How can you take it seriously?

In all fairness, though, I cannot deny that over the years I've made a lot of fans. For example, I know for a fact I have one fan in Bulgaria. He emailed to tell me he'd heard my songs in a television movie called *I Me Wed*. Who knew it would air in Bulgaria?

I also happen to know that I have three fans in Tel Aviv, two fans in California, about eight fans in Boston, a small group of four to five people in New York City, and about two hundred townsfolk who showed up to my gig in a medieval town in eastern France several years ago.

If someone says to you, "I'm a fan," it usually means they are not going to kill you and you should take it as a compliment.

Sometimes the audience will clap loudly after you play a song. I always wonder, how long do you wait before saying, "thank you" into the microphone. Do you wait until their applause has petered out? Do you wait several seconds? Is there time for a sip of vodka? Or do you say "thank you" while they're still clapping? I still do not know.

Sometimes when you finish your song, they will whistle, or holler, or yell something like "*Whoo hooo!*" Do not be scared when this happens. Also, do no not take it as a signal to take off your clothing.

Alternatively, there is always one person in the audience whose cell phone goes off during your performance. Do *not* let this distract you from the task at hand. Also, pay no attention to the guy in the front row who's yawning in the middle of your poignant ballad. Just be glad no one has thrown any tomatoes, finish your set as quickly as you can, and then weep in the alley.

The best and most wonderful thing that can happen in a show is when someone from the audience comes up to you afterwards and tells you that your song made them cry. This makes you cry, and you find yourselves embracing each other, rocking slowly from foot to foot, and weeping into each other's shoulders.

It is your fans who will let you know you've made the right choices in your songs. They are the ones who will make you feel less crazy for having the dream of making music! And, unlike the guy from the record label who never returns your emails, they are the ones who will "get" you. As long as you have them, you are not on your own as you travel the often lost and lonely path of an independent singer-songwriter.

Banter

WHAT IS "BANTER"? Dictionary.com says it is "an exchange of light, playful, teasing remarks," or "good natured raillery." If I knew what "raillery" meant, it would help even more.

When they're onstage, folksingers love to use banter between songs. This differs from the rock stars who, at best, mumble a short "thank ye, thank ye" between songs, and usually it is in a sexy British accent. Have you ever noticed how rock stars are more mysterious the *less* they say?

But folkies know that using banter is a great way to win over their audience, break the ice, and let the crowd get to know them better.

I once knew a guy from Nashville who would spend half an hour backstage writing out and memorizing his banter before his shows. He was good at it but he sure took his time.

That raises the question: How long should you banter in between songs? Rule of thumb: When audience members start to boo or talk amongst themselves, you will know your banter has gone on too long. This is your cue to swing your guitar back in place—immediately—and start singing again, like there's no tomorrow.

A friend of mine says to just act natural in your banter. What I like to do is talk about my relationship issues with the audience. "Do you think I should leave my boyfriend?" I will ask them. "Or do you think I should not leave him? Stay or go?" I figure someone might have some good advice for me, so why not put it out there?

"Leave him!" some guy will yell. Then I will give him a free CD at the end of the show. I always find their suggestions so helpful!

One time I played in a bar in Manhattan and Tony Bennett was in the audience. That is, he was in the audience watching his daughter's jazz set, right before mine. He took off in his limo before I got onstage. That night, I decided to deliver some friendly banter in between my songs. But I must have gone on a bit too long because my own manager called out from the audience, "Okay, next!" It's a good thing Tony Bennett missed it.

I once saw a folksinger tell an epic story about his life: "I grew up in Minneapolis . . . [nine minutes pass] . . . and I wrote this song when my mother left us . . ." On it went. It was a disaster. A drunk woman in the audience began to cry. A guy in the front row began to snore.

So you see, it is important to learn just what is the appropriate length for your banter. Also, put some thought into your content. Stay away from inappropriate jokes. Never mock a member of your audience. For example, don't yell, "Nice hairdo!" at someone, I learned.

Try not to read your banter from notes. Memorize it until it flows naturally. You can introduce your next song if you want, or leave them guessing. Try not to tell the same story twice (you might have fans come to see your show in a different town) and remember: When your own manager yells, "Next!" it's time to play.

How to Get into This Lousy Business

S OME OF YOU MIGHT be wondering how I got into this lousy business in the first place. Well, it all started when I went down to a crossroads and I sold my soul to the devil. Wait a minute. That was Robert Johnson.

Actually, I was born on October 9, 1970, at Toronto General Hospital with so much hair the nurses kept putting it up in bows. I was born with a mullet, which, as you know, just screams "music career."

I grew up with family jamborees in our living room. My mother and Auntie Carol would double on the piano. Auntie Carol was a robust woman who sometimes threatened to push my mother right off the bench, but somehow they made it work. My grandfather and great-uncle were on violins (though it took them over half an hour to tune). There were various cousins on guitars, my brother on mandolin, the occasional accordion or harmonica, and me in my four-year-old mullet, wearing my American-flag overalls, skipping around and beating a tambourine to "When the saints (*oh, when the saints!*) go marchin' in." I was enthralled by the call and response.

I heard everything from Broadway musicals to protest songs. The best were the Russian folk tunes, when the violins got fast and manic at the end. One time, I walked into the tiny first-floor bathroom of our house to find my grandfather and great-uncle on their violins, and my cousin Shula, with her long brown hippie hair, strumming her guitar on the toilet seat.

They were squished there, playing the sixties folk song "Donna, Donna." I must have looked confused because one of them said: "The acoustics are better in here."

As I was growing up, music was a river coursing through my veins. One morning we read in the paper that auditions were being held in New York for the Broadway musical *Annie*. I pleaded with my parents to let me audition.

They didn't take me seriously. My dad, a doctor, was on the phone, talking in some kind of medical gibberish. I could never understand what he was saying but I figured it was important. My mother was busy with my younger sister, a quirky little Fraggle Rock creature who wore a Raggedy Ann wig for most of her childhood. She would come to my school with my mother, who played piano for our choir. I was so embarrassed by that wig I would hide.

At ten years old, I wrote my first song. I'd become obsessed with the theme song from the Neil Simon movie *The Goodbye Girl*, starring Richard Dreyfuss. I recorded the theme from our television onto a tape recorder. I listened over and over until I fell asleep. That night I dreamed of a melody that I recognized as my own. When I woke up I could still hear it in my head so I ran downstairs to figure it out on the piano. Turns out, it was a mash-up of chords from "Goodbye Girl." Next, I wrote the words. When I played it for my piano teacher, he loved it so much he made photocopies for all of his students.

My first brush with showbiz was in seventh grade when I starred in *Joseph and the Amazing Technicolor Dreamcoat*. I must have wowed the music and drama directors with my audition piece—it was "You're Never Fully Dressed Without a Smile," from *Annie*, with the whole hat-and-cane routine. The next day I went to look at the audition list. It read: "Kathy Goldman—Joseph."

To say I was perturbed would be an understatement! I knew it was the lead but for the life of me, I couldn't understand how I was supposed to play a boy when I was a girl. After some prodding and convincing from the drama director, I went ahead with it and, might I say, downright stole the show, which ran for two nights in the basement of a synagogue.

I was such a hit that the rabbi asked me to come back and sing from the Torah during the High Holidays. In fact, I was so passionate about my role as Joseph that they'd find me walking down the hallways at school wearing my Technicolor dreamcoat, which was really just a large, colourful woollen cape that hung around my shoulders.

In 1981, at age eleven, I showed up to school in a perm and a pink satin shorts onesie. My friends and I were listening to "The Best of Times" by Styx, and "Open Arms" by Journey. They were big, melodic, power ballads that lit me on fire, informing the kinds of songs I wanted to write one day. I dreamed of being high on a stage, lunging at a microphone, and flipping my hair up and down.

By the time I got to high school, word on the street was I could sing. I had morphed into a flower child with long, wavy hair and embroidered Mexican cotton blouses. I joined a Grateful Dead cover band, even though I had no idea who the Grateful Dead were. We called ourselves the Smoking Coconuts. I still have no idea why. Maybe because we were a bunch of hash-smoking postmodern hippies acting like a bunch of coconuts.

We developed quite a following, mostly because people came to our shows on acid and we were the trip. (Later on, I genuinely came to love the Grateful Dead and found myself right at home floating high on mushrooms through concert parking lots in cities throughout America.)

Every show, my band would let me do a solo. It was either the blues song "Baby, What You Want Me to Do," or "I Wish I Knew (How It Would Feel to Be Free)," by Nina Simone. I'd play the keyboard. The Nina Simone song became my trademark. It was a favourite request at parties, high school talent shows, and especially the family jamboree. I'd build up the final verse with gusto and my auntie Carol would shout: "Now give it to 'em!" or "You know what to do!"

That summer at camp was the first time I heard Bob Dylan's song "Don't Think Twice, It's All Right." I almost fell off the top bunk in our cabin. His fingerpicking style and melody just plain knocked me for a loop. I'd never heard anything like it but, at the same time, it was like I had always been waiting to hear a song like that. It was otherworldly.

At nineteen, I flunked out of the dance program at York University, and then the music department, and spent the rest of the year on my sofa in my first apartment, at Davisville and Yonge. I listened to every single Joni Mitchell album in the world. I'd yodel along, trying to emulate her voice, or just lie there weeping. If only Joni knew she'd saved me from a monumental depressive episode that year.

In my twenties, I was writing all kinds of songs about not getting married, wild ex-boyfriends, and taking Prozac. I started to perform them at the open mike every Monday night at the Free Times Café. To my surprise, people actually didn't hate them. This led to my own gigs. Hundreds, maybe thousands of them, over twenty years.

And now with four albums, two songs covered by famous artists, a high-profile New York manager, about eight fans in Boston and one in Bulgaria, two band mates who made fun of my outfits, three Finalist wins from a Nashville competition (even though they never gave me any prizes), a house concert in the freezing cold on a dairy farm in Manitoba, a small tour in some medieval town in France where they showered me with baguette sandwiches, at least twelve placements in movies and television, several radio interviews where I got to wear my sweatpants, various rocker boyfriends who never made me a coffee in the morning, and a regular cheque in the mail for $23.32, I have to admit I haven't done so bad for myself as an independent singer-songwriter.

Vocal Warm-Ups

SOME PEOPLE MIGHT WONDER what songwriters do all day. "What do you *d-o-o-o-o* all day?" they will say.

Well, for one thing, each and every day, songwriters must do their vocal warm-ups.

I've heard a lot of stories about singers damaging their voices. Often they have no training and just go for it, singing night after night, relying on innate talent. Soon they're seeing doctors, coaches, and other therapists to painstakingly rebuild their voices. It's important to develop the strength and stamina you need to perform and, especially, to tour. The best way to do this, in my experience, is to work with a vocal teacher.

I've had a number of coaches throughout my career. It can take time to find the teacher who's right for you. I've had nine. I am grateful to all of them since I came away from each and every one with valuable tips.

My first teacher taught me "monkey sound," which, when you really get into it, makes you curl your fingers under your armpits and jump from foot to foot as you say: "whohh-whohh-whohh."

Then there was "bear voice." This meant writhing on the carpet, sticking out my tongue, and, yes, roaring like a bear.

It's difficult to maintain decorum around your teacher during these practices. What refinement you have falls away as you growl and grunt, and occasionally drool. I admit I sometimes felt a bit silly writing my cheque at the end of a lesson, after I'd been writhing and rolling on the floor for an hour, but for the most part I entrusted my beloved teachers with the greatest confidence.

One had me sing like a baby. Another had me whine like a dog, furling my lips at the corners, making my eyebrows into an inverted V as I imitated a dog seeking attention. My teacher liked to demonstrate the whining dog himself, and he did it with exceptional ability. The other dogs in the building howled in response. People in the street looked up at the window.

It was my whining-dog teacher who put my weekly lesson on tape so that I could practise on my own. One day, leaving the studio with my producers in the car, I turned on the ignition and my tape started to play. "Neeeeyyyeeeeeewwwwwwwwwww" came my voice through the speakers, followed by the whining, growling, and baby sounds, the monkey "whohhs," some raven "cawwws."

My producers howled. One was laughing so hard he began to snort. You would have thought it was the funniest thing they'd ever heard. What they did not appreciate was just how committed I was to my vocal practice.

In fact, I was so dedicated, I'd worked out which rooms and at what times I could practise in my apartment without my neighbours hearing (the shower was good). I did not want a reputation as the crazy person in my building, or to sound like I was being attacked by an intruder, or smuggling exotic animals.

The voice is a muscle, my teachers would say: "You must become a vocal athlete!" A vocal warm-up in the morning can help you wake up, improve your mood, and prepare you for when you sing your material. Train it right and you will be able to count on your voice during your performance.

Finding Your Look

I F YOU'RE GOING TO be a songwriter working in the music industry, you might want to spend some time thinking about your look.

Have you ever wondered how some people find their look much more easily than others do? They just throw on a cap, or a cowboy hat, or swing a cape around their shoulders, and they're good to go. Elvis had a look. So did Madonna. The Beatles had a number of compelling hairdos over their career. I myself have still have not found my look, although I am open to suggestions.

Don't get me wrong! I have tried a few numbers, like when I wore a puffy white and generously sized crinoline lace tutu for one of my opening nights. My drummer at the time really took offence to it. "You looked ridiculous!" he said. "And my friends thought so, too."

Well, I thought that was *very* unkind. Especially since I was paying him for the gig *plus* the rehearsals. I just don't know why some people try to knock you down. Maybe it's because they're mean. Maybe they're jealous. Anyway, like *he* was one to talk, wearing those ridiculous, ugly thin black nylon drummer slippers every time he sat at the drum set. Was he drumming or was he going windsurfing?

For the past few years I'd been threatening to wear an oversized curly black Cher wig to promote my new album. However, my friends were baffled: "What does it mean?" they would ask me.

"What? It's a character," I would tell them.

To be honest, I'm still not sure of the meaning of the Cher wig. All I know is I wore it for one gig and it was so hot under the lights that my makeup began to run and I looked like something from a horror show. I will never wear that wig again, although I do keep it in my closet.

When I lived in Boston, I tried Elvis, the Vegas years, but that was a hard one to pull off. With long sideburns, people tend to mistake you for a man. I also wore an eye patch for one engagement but people couldn't decide if I was mysterious or if I was really missing an eye.

I gave the David Bowie unitard a whirl for a recent concert. Again, not an easy ensemble. I looked more like a beached whale in feather earrings.

Maybe one day it will come to me.

Perhaps my greatest stunt was a photo shoot as a burlesque dancer. I used it for a poster to promote a show at Hugh's Room in Toronto. I was a little more plump than usual, what with living in America and all.

The night of the show, a fellow songwriter raised a fuss: "Why would you wear such a silly getup?" He was very upset about the way I was marketing myself. It's not like *he* wore that stupid outfit.

What I'm trying say is, you shouldn't let other people's opinions interfere with your dress choices. Songwriters need to express themselves freely! I've had managers tell me to wear my hair up, wear my hair down, wear a hat, or don't wear a hat. Do not listen to them! Did they write these songs? As singer-songwriters and musicians, it is in our nature to want to stand out from the crowd. So pull on those tight leather pants, bust out your chest hair, and grow that handlebar moustache. Dare to be different. Most of all, and remember this, just be you.

Gimmicks & Special Talents

ONCE SAW A GUY who could sing, play guitar, blow on a harmonica, bang on a marching drum, crash cymbals, and tap dance, all at the same time. All that while wearing a cowboy hat that never fell off! How did he know when to strum, tap, blow, crash, drum, or sing in a coordinated fashion? Then every once in a while, he would put down his guitar and juggle some oranges. At the same time as he was tap dancing!

It made me wonder: Was he a singer-songwriter or was he trying out for the circus? I mean, if you're a good songwriter and performer, why do you need to rely on gimmicks?

On the other hand, what if you do possess some extraordinary talent? Shouldn't you use it during your show? I've seen American singer-songwriter Christine Lavin twirl a baton in between songs. It kept her song format from getting routine and demonstrated her unique baton-twirling ability.

A friend said he knows a guy who can put a whole harmonica in his mouth and still play it. I questioned this: "What do you mean, he put the whole harmonica in his mouth? He'd have to have a pretty big mouth, don't you think? Just how wide was his mouth?"

"Well," my friend said, "part of the harmonica was sticking out."

"Which part?" I asked. "Just the corner or also a few notes?"

"About an inch," he said.

Apparently this guy could play just as well with practically the whole harmonica in his mouth as when he held it outside his mouth. That is a special talent. I'd go to his show just to see if he swallowed it.

My mother has the freakish gift of being able to play the piano while sitting backwards on the piano bench. She calls it being ambidextrous. If only she could have passed this talent on to me. I could use such a gimmick in my shows. Now *that* would be rock 'n' roll!

Use your special talents for your show but whatever you do, please, no xylophone. How many *god*damn times do I have to hear another xylophone in a song? It's used *again* and *again*, and anyhow, what's so special about a xylophone? Why not spoons or an old washboard? Children play xylophones! They are meant for children! Stop trying to be *cute* by plinking delicately on the keys of your xylophone.

And no megaphones either. Why use a megaphone when you have a microphone? We can hear you! Are you playing a show or auctioning farm equipment?

In sum, gimmicks are not necessary for your show but if you can play the piano with your toes, that could be memorable.

Promo

YOU KNOW WHAT THEY SAY: "Promo! Promo! Promo!" And that is exactly what you should be doing as a songwriter, all the time, fearlessly, and without regrets.

What I'm trying to say is, if you want to put posters of yourself with a come-hither look all around your city, that's your prerogative. Just be prepared for family, friends, bosses, ex-lovers, and all of your peers to see them. If your friends and relatives do see your poster on a lamppost downtown, and they ask: "Why aren't you smiling in your picture?" Just tell them: "Nobody ever smiles in rock 'n' roll."

I mean, have you ever seen a rock star smile in one of their photos? Never! The thing is to look deep and mysterious. Think of a young Bob Dylan in sunglasses and a black leather jacket. In general, you want to give the impression that you're really pissed off about something and that you're mean as hell.

Obviously, you will have to do a photo shoot at some point. This means two and a half hours of hair and makeup that will leave you so stressed and exhausted that by the time the photographer starts snapping, you'll look like you've seen a ghost. And I don't care what anyone says: Women, for crying out loud, put on some makeup for your photo shoots and videos! Do you want to look like you're missing a mouth? Most of all, and remember this: never underestimate the value of a good lipstick.

Here are some dos and don'ts for promoting your music:

- *Don't* drive around your city, town, village, or shtetl with the windows down and a taxi billboard of your face on the roof of the car while you play your album at full volume.

- *Don't* drive slowly in your car with your new album playing at full volume while you yell at people through a megaphone to buy your new album. Or else, you *could* do this, but it might count as a traffic violation.

- *Do* contact local radio stations to see if they might be interested in interviewing you. Remember, wearing sweatpants or pajamas is fine. It's radio! No one will see you!

- *Don't* peddle your CD door-to-door. People might think you're poor and hungry and send you away with a can of soup or a Bible, or something like that.

- *Do* hire a good publicist. Press reviews in magazines and newspapers are good to have.

- *Do* send your album to every folk, college, and indie radio DJ introduced to you by Google. Make sure it is digitally encoded. Ask if they would prefer a hard or electronic copy. And send along a friendly note with your photo and contact information.

- *Do* wear whatever you feel represents you and your music in your photos and on your album cover. But try not to be confusing. For example, dressing like one of the members of Kiss might not give off the right vibe for an acoustic folk recording.

- *Don't* stand on street corners in a Cher wig and American-flag overalls yelling at people to buy your CD: "You can pay me anything you want. Just pay me . . . *something*, at least!"

- *Do* contact anyone you know who has connections to anybody who might be able to help with your career. Worst-case scenario, they'll never return your emails but you will get used to that soon enough.

- *Do* use quotes to promote your music, especially if they're from famous people. If you're really stuck for a quote, you can always make one up. For example, you could write, "Kat Goldman is a Canadian flower," says Artie Feldman in *Hipster Illustrated*, even though Artie Feldman doesn't exist, and neither does his magazine. I mean, who's going to know?

- *Do* use social media sites like Facebook, Twitter, and Instagram to promote your music, never mind that I have no idea how to use Instagram and no one looks at Twitter anymore.
- Finally, and most important, *don't* be shy about getting your music out there!

CDs

RECENTLY DID A SHOW at the Tranzac Club in Toronto. A woman came up to me at the bar before my set. "Hey, Kat!" she said. "I finally get to see you play! I've been a fan for a long time. I've brought some of my friends tonight." They loved the show but neither the woman nor her friends wanted a CD.

Later, a pair of younger women stopped me. "Kat, you were really great tonight! You remind me of Stevie Nicks!"

"Wow," I said. "Thank you so much! Stevie Nicks? I love her! Hey, listen, I have some CDs for sale. Would you like one?" They just sat on their bar stools and shook their heads.

"Is it because you don't have a CD player? Oh, I get it. Nobody has CD players anymore," I said. They looked like deer in headlights.

"How much are they?" one of them finally asked.

"Twenty," I said. "Or fifteen, if you like. I try to base it on what people can afford. Ten? How about ten? Ten dollars? Five? Tell you what." I reached into my bag and grabbed a CD. "You can take one for free."

"Are you sure?"

"Just play it for your friends," I said. I figure that's the way to start a revolution. One person plays it for their friends, and that person plays it for *their* friends, and so on.

I don't get it. How come I can never sell any of my CDs? Sometimes I can't even give one away for free! Whether it's at a tiny coffee house or a massive folk festival, nobody ever wants a copy.

Years ago, I had my first album signed to a folk music distribution company in Canada. This meant the company would get my CD in record stores all over the country. It was a good feeling until six months later a large box with one hundred CDs was returned to me along with a brief note:

"We apologize for this inconvenience but we've gone out of business."

I guess I don't have to tell you that after a while all this rejection can really start to get you down.

Of course people now grab music right off their phones or computers. They can stream whatever they like, from all kinds of sites, and for not much money at all. They can go on iTunes where they don't have to buy an album, just one song. (That's ninety-nine cents for Apple, one cent for me.)

A lot of music is also available for free on YouTube. You can hear almost anything you want. I've had over 83,000 plays of "Annabel" on YouTube but you think I get paid for it?

So now what am I supposed to do with all the CDs I've had manufactured? I have twenty boxes of *The Great Disappearing Act* sitting in my parents' basement.

Don't worry. I devise new strategies for moving CDs all the time. I now take a copy onstage with me. Somewhere in the middle of my set, I will pick it up and begin to fondle it in front of the audience. "I have my CDs here for sale tonight, folks," I will say, caressing the rim. "They're twenty dollars but I'm *very* flexible."

I'm sure you know that CDs are becoming obsolete. Soon they'll be a thing of the past, if they aren't already. Fortunately, they have other uses. They make great coasters. Folkies like to roll joints on them. I've used them to pick up men (it actually worked, once).

Like What You Like

AFTER A SHORT STINT in the dance department at York University in 1989, I switched to the music department. One day, I was sitting around the college pub with some of the jazz guys. That old question arose: "What album would you want to have with you on a desert island?" We went around the table. One guy said, *Porgy and Bess*. Another said, Coltrane's *A Love Supreme*. I said: "Anything by Simon and Garfunkel."

The jazz cats loved that one. "Simon and Garfunkel. Bwahahahaha!"

But to this day, I hold my ground. First of all, there's always something so familiar about Simon and Garfunkel. Their music was the soundtrack to my childhood. They remind me of sitting in the cabin on a rainy day in summer. When I hear their music, I feel as if I'm coming home.

Take "The Boxer," for example. I've never had a clue what the song is about. Is it a man? A dog? But I know every word, and the frolicking fingerpicking pattern at the start and those bouncing bass notes on the guitar just make my soul happy. It's also the perfect campfire song. Everyone can join in on the "Lie la lies." And who doesn't love singing the "lie la lies?" 'Course, there won't be anyone to sing them with you on the desert island, but you can still do them in your head.

Then there's "The Sound of Silence." Such a sad, deep, and powerful lament: "Hello darkness my old friend." Simon and Garfunkel really could have depressed us but instead they invite us in and make it a beautiful, even uplifting experience. It's a soothing cup of cocoa on a winter's day. In fact, that's what I should say when my depressions hit: "Hello darkness, my old friend." Perhaps it would lighten the mood.

And what about "Bridge Over Troubled Water?" Epic! Brings tears to my eyes just thinking about it. Soon as I hear Art Garfunkel's soft and careful pipes, I get the shivers: the build up of the gospel piano, the strings coming in gently towards the middle, and the drums at the end: "Sail on silver girl . . . / All your dreams are on their way." It's the ultimate song about empathy. "I'm sailing right behind." Anyone who will lay himself "down / Like a bridge over troubled water" is a good friend to have. And that's what Simon and Garfunkel's music has always been to me—a good old friend.

Now what the jazz big shots at York didn't ask me was what food I would want on my desert island. And to that, I would say challah French toast, because it's sweet, and soft, and would be easy to chew when the scurvy sets in.

Keep Your Day Job

I F YOU'RE THINKING OF working in the music industry as a singer-songwriter, you might want to keep your day job. Truth is, I've never made a dime in this business. I've lost more money making albums than I've ever made back in CD or streaming sales.

As an independent singer-songwriter, you're expected to pay for your band, your producer, the mixing and mastering of your recording, your manufacturing, your album artwork, a publicist, your website—and, well, the list just goes on and on.

At this point, I don't even view my CDs as currency. I see them more like calling cards, something to give people with my contact information and my face on them. Except on my latest album cover I'm wearing an oversized curly black Cher wig so it might be hard to identify me.

In fact, I give more of my CDs away for free than I sell. I've given my CDs to the plumber, the cleaning lady, the two women who work at the convenience store down the street, the handyman, the waitress at Sunset Grill, the sushi delivery guy, and on Christmas Day I even gave one to some woman who started speaking to me on Yonge Street because she was distraught that her mother was in the hospital.

I figure some of those people might actually have played it, that is, if anyone owns a CD player anymore. Maybe one of my songs reached them, spoke to them, touched them on some level. And at least I'm getting my music "out there," as they say, meaning out of the boxes in my parents' basement.

Every two months I get a cheque in the mail for $23.32. Sometimes I neglect to cash it because I just find it so amusing to look at a cheque for so little money! Those are the proceeds from single downloads of my songs through iTunes and Spotify.

Four times a year, I get a slightly larger royalty cheque for song placements in television shows and movies, and for replays of my song "Annabel." I was never good at math but the amounts are not enough to live on. l still consider it an improvement on receiving my night's wages from a smelly old passed hat or a tip jar.

Music is the kind of business that demands you have a Plan B. Mine is a pact I have with one of my friends: if he ever finds me pushing a shopping cart with all my belongings, wearing painted-on eyebrows and a smear of lipstick, high on Listerine, he will take me in for a spaghetti dinner and we'll talk about the ol' times.

Here are just *some* ideas for day jobs I've tried, which you might also consider, as you go along your path of developing your songwriting career:

1. Watering and cutting sunflower sprouts on an organic sprout farm.
2. Cleaning bathrooms in a massage parlor. (Remember: one squirt of Scrubbing Bubbles goes a looong way.)
3. Internet porn agency (What? I was just the secretary!)
4. Scooping ice cream.
5. Busking on a street corner in a Cher wig and American-flag overalls.

The Dangling Carrot

THERE WILL BE THOSE in the music business—agents, managers, and record label people—who will dangle a big fat orange carrot before you. They will entice you with all kinds of things like record deals, high-profile gigs, a tour, or, in my case, an appearance on a national TV talk show.

I was told by my first manager to go out and buy a new outfit for my TV appearance. I purchased a red satin sports jumpsuit that made me look like Ben Stiller in *The Royal Tenenbaums*, matched with a pair of open-toed platform Miu Miu disco sandals.

A week went by, and then another, with no word about the talk show. It never happened, and my management contract ended not long after that. My hopes for massive recognition were dashed but to this day I thank *god* I never wore that red satin jumpsuit on national television.

Many years ago, I landed a high-profile gig at an outdoor Toronto festival through somebody else's manager. I thanked him profusely. "Just don't suck!" he grumbled, leaning back in his chair and crossing his legs on top of his desk.

Well, suck I didn't! My band totally rocked it out, and the crowd went wild. I was bombarded with fans backstage asking for autographs. And then a stout blond woman with short hair came running at me.

"You were s-o-o-o wonderful!" she bubbled. "I just l-o-o-o-ved your voice! I work at the law office of so-and-so. We've had several artists signed by major labels, and we would l-o-o-o-ve to have you come in and talk about management!"

A week later, hopeful and doe-eyed, I showed up with my guitar wearing the tightest white T-shirt I could find. Except when the lawyer appeared, he didn't ask me to play my songs. He just stood in the doorway and said: "I listened to your album and, well, there are no hits."

No hits? Everyone who heard the album counted at least five hits! I guess at the end of the day it all comes down to taste. That and maybe who you sleep with. Thankfully, I've never made that particular compromise. The only time I went to bed with someone to get something I wanted was with my masseur in Mexico and only because my neck was really sore after the long flight and he had these great big healing hands.

Another time, I drove seven hours in a snowstorm because someone had dangled in front of me the opportunity to open for an American folk music celebrity. When I arrived at the bar, his tour manager approached me: "I'm really sorry, there must have been a mistake. So-and-so doesn't like to have openers. But I'll tell you what. Maybe if I tell him you're hot, he'll reconsider."

"Well," I said, "can you please tell Mr. So-and-So that I just drove seven hours in a snowstorm to get here?"

I went to my room, rolled out my yoga mat, sat on it, and had a good cry. Afterwards,

I called my mother from a payphone.

"This is such a lousy business you're in," she said. "Can't you work with children or something like that?"

I had another good cry. Later, I bumped into my erstwhile headliner near the dressing room. He offered me Smarties from a bowl and asked if I would like to sit with him on the sofa.

"I was supposed to open for you tonight," I said.

"Ohhh!" he said. "You were the opener! Yeah, I'm really sorry about that. My manager made a mistake. I usually don't have openers."

Then he said, "If you *were* to get up, how long a set would you want to play?"

"Give me fifteen minutes?"

I played four songs and wowed his audience. The following morning we met by chance over breakfast and became fast friends. He and his tour manager both told me they had loved my album *The Great Disappearing Act* after listening to it on their drive home. I drove off on a high, and never heard from famous Mr. So-and-So again.

I guess whatever life-changing things the dangling carrot was supposed to bring were not my true destiny. I would never have made a good famous person, anyway. The paramedics would have found me alone and drugged in my Los Angeles pool, floating on an inflatable frog.

I figure being famous isn't everything it's cracked up to be. You'd never be able to just go to a movie, or buy a pair of jeans, or do anything *normal* like that again. And what *is* success, at the end of the day? Something you have to define for yourself, on your own terms. Maybe it's having one person come to you at the end of your show and tell you that your song brought them to tears.

Beware the dangling carrot. Do it your way instead, and don't let the bastards get you down.

Opening Act

THERE'S NOTHING WRONG WITH being the opening act. In fact, it's one of the best gigs a songwriter can have! Heck, I've practically made a career of being the opening act.

First of all, having shared the stage with someone famous gives you clout. Plus, the venue might treat you really well. They might leave chips and dip and soda for you in your dressing room.

Once in a fancy New York nightclub they gave me a full spread: chocolate, salsa, Tostitos, wine, the works. Everything about it was first class, until I turned around and saw the male wait staff talking with each other in their underwear. That's when I realized my dressing room wasn't a dressing room at all. It was the male staff's locker room. I didn't mind.

I've opened for so many famous people I've forgotten some of their names! But there are also some I remember: Eric Andersen, Martin Sexton, the Strawbs, Dar Williams, Jonatha Brooke, Al Stewart, Colin Hay, and Midge Ure, to name a few.

Playing the opening act before a high-profile songwriter or band forces you to prepare well in advance and work hard towards your gig. It makes you step it up a notch, and challenges you to become a stronger performer. Your confidence grows from knowing that for that evening, on that stage, you will be in the same league as your co-bill.

There are other perks to being the opening act. It's always great exposure for you. It looks great on your bio, and suddenly your friends and family will think you're really cool because somehow you landed a gig with a famous person.

Forget right away the idea that the opening act is considered lesser than the main act. I saw REO Speedwagon open for Chicago, and REO stole the show. They were on fire! Was it because they tour more frequently than Chicago and were effortless in their performance? Chicago seemed strained and slow to get started. People were impatient, getting up from their seats to buy popcorn. They didn't even play "Hard to Say I'm Sorry" until the very end! (But you know who was sobbing and flicking her Bic when they finally did.)

Think of your opening set as a great opportunity to win over a new audience, one that was built by your main act. You might really connect with them and they with you. With luck, the crowd will share your aesthetic. Opening for Dar Williams is always a treat for me because her audience genuinely loves singer-songwriter folk music. Thus, your music might totally complement your co-bill and the night could go swimmingly. Or you could be paired with a thrash metal band. Then you're really screwed. (If I dived backwards off the stage, would that audience even catch me?)

You might want to listen to the main act's music as a courtesy, and so you'll have something to talk about should you meet backstage. Don't be afraid to gush. Hopefully they will be nice to you. They might check in with you at the end of the night to see how the venue treated you, and that you got paid. Colin Hay came up to me after our show and asked me if I had been treated nicely by the club. I wanted to say yes but he was about eight feet tall, so far over my head that I could only look up, smile, and wave at him way up there.

Alternatively, your main acts might not be nice at all. They might be real assholes, like the famous guy I opened for at Hugh's Room. I should have known after what happened on the sofa in the dressing room before the show. I first thought it was an insect crawling on me but when I went to brush it away, I realized it was my co-bill, kissing my neck and whispering sweet nothings into my ear: "Would you like to go to the movies sometime?"

He later asked if he could use my keyboard for one of his numbers. Of course I let him use it. Except he duct-taped my keyboard pedal to one exact spot on the floor to suit his posture. The spot was so far away from where my short legs reached that when it was my turn to play, I kept sliding off the bench and under the keyboard. I felt like I was doing the limbo! And guess who had to pay for the keyboard rental at the end of the night?

The odd bad experience notwithstanding, there's no shame in playing the opening set. It's usually a win-win. Get as many of those gigs as you can. You might make some new fans, and, who knows, you might even get a tour out of it.

To Tour, or Not to Tour

WHILE OTHER SINGER-SONGWRITERS are slogging it out on the festival circuit or driving through blizzards to bars in remote parts of the country, I am at home, cozy in my apartment, wearing my red fuzzy robe. There is no place I would rather be!

Why herniate your discs schlepping a guitar and heavy keyboard from one city to the next, day after day?

Why bother getting lost—alone—in a rental truck in which your feet can barely reach the pedals, along some highway in rural Manitoba—in the dead of winter; I'm talking minus thirty degrees in the Prairies—to play a house concert? Actually, it was in a barn on a dairy farm, in front of a bunch of elderly dairy farmers sitting on hay bundles. Do you have any idea how cold and dry it is at minus thirty degrees? You open your mouth and all that comes out is "ehk-ehhhk."

I've spent endless hours in a car only to wind up strumming heartfelt ballads to a gaggle of men in baseball caps who can't take their eyes from the game on the television hanging over my head at the bar.

I've travelled to darkest Rochester, the university cafeteria, only to compete, in front of three students, with the noise from the cappuccino maker.

"I thought you had to *tour* your new album," my cousin said to me recently. My cousin thinks he is so clever.

Who can afford to tour? Especially after the enormous expense of recording an album. I never know if I'm going to break even on a gig, let alone make a profit. And that's without bringing my band.

"I'd rather stick pins and needles in my eyes," I told my cousin. "And anyhow, I could never leave my dog for that long."

Instead, I've made my most recent album a stay-at-home, Web-based operation, mailing out CDs, doing phone interviews, and releasing my video for "Release Me" over YouTube and Facebook, all the while, of course, wearing the red fuzzy robe.

Booking Agents

THERE'S NOT MUCH I can say about booking agents. Not even what their function might be, because I've never had one myself. I've always booked my own shows.

Which reminds me, never call up the guy who books the Iron Horse Music Hall in Northampton, Massachusetts. It's one of those so-hip-it-hurts venues that only wants high-profile acts. My conversation with the guy at the Iron Horse Music Hall went like this:

"Hi! My name is Kat Goldman, and I'm a singer-songwriter from Canada. I'm wondering if you might be interested in booking a show sometime."

"I only book shows through managers," the booker grumbled. But at the time, I didn't have a manager.

"Oh, okay, well, thank you very much for your time," I said, and hung up the phone, feeling dejected, wondering all over again if I had a future in the business.

I let a few minutes go by and picked up the phone again.

"Hullo?" I said, making my voice low and manly. "Hullo, yuuus, this is Kat Goldman's manager, and I'd like to book something for her."

There was a pause.

"Aren't you the person who just phoned me a few minutes ago?"

"No? I'm Kat Goldman's *manager*," I said, trying to make my voice lower and deeper.

"You're the same person that just phoned me five minutes ago—and now you're disguising your voice to act like you're her manager!" He was shouting at me.

"I see, well, nice talking with you and I hope you have a very nice day," I said in my regular voice and quickly hung up. That was the last time I tried to book a show at the Iron Horse Music Hall.

Bartenders and Bar Owners

Why do bartenders and bar owners make musicians pay for their drinks at the end of the night? I'll never understand it. We're bringing business into their bar. Shouldn't we be treated with a little more respect? And how about a cheeseburger every once in a while?

Bartenders and bar owners like to complain about where we put our gear. Even after we've driven seven hours in a snowstorm to get there. How about starting with "Welcome! We're excited to have you play tonight!" Better than shooting us dirty looks from behind the bar like we're a bunch of low-lifes just off the street. Songwriters have feelings, too, you know.

Once I was waiting for the sound check, and I asked the bartender for a glass of water.

"Sorry," he said. "Bar's not open yet."

"But I'm the main act tonight."

"Come back in twenty minutes."

"But . . . I just want water," I said.

What a jerk. Rather like the bar owners who demand a cut of our CD sales at the end of the night. Did they record that CD? Did they write those songs?

Still worse are the bartenders and bar owners who insist that we plug the food on their menu, or tell our fans to buy more beer between songs. That is not our job! We've got other things to think about. We have to set up, get through sound check, greet people, sometimes work the door, sometimes work the soundboard, prepare mentally, and put on a good show for you all. *You* sell your goddamn beers! And give me one for free while you're at it.

Fame

A LOT OF PEOPLE GET into the music business hoping to meet fame. There were a few times in my career when I almost became famous.

Let's see, there was the time I was playing in a bar when an A&R (artists and repertoire) guy from Sony records came up to me. I was twenty-eight years old. He said he loved my song "Annabel" and wanted to sign me to his label. This was back when labels were still signing artists.

The Sony guy asked me for a recording of my songs. I didn't have one at the time so I went into the studio for several months and made a cassette tape with my first six original songs. The last was "Annabel."

Sadly, the deal with Sony never worked out but at least I had a cassette tape I could peddle at shows.

Six months later, I was at my weekly gig, singing and playing guitar to customers in the fruits and vegetables section at Loblaws supermarket. Well, wouldn't you know, there was the guy from Sony, pushing a shopping cart one floor below me. I watched with dread as he rode up the escalator towards me on the second-floor balcony.

"Hey Kat," he said. "Listen, I'm sorry, again, that I couldn't do more for your career."

"That's okay," I said, and went back to singing "The Sound of Silence" to a woman sniffing a cantaloupe.

Another time I almost became famous was when a high-profile manager took a plane from New York City to catch my show in Buffalo. He asked me if I would sign a three-year contract right there on the spot.

I did and my new management started flying me to New York all the time. They had me showcase in front of record labels all over Manhattan for about two years. But that was when the record companies really did stop signing artists. We never landed that elusive and now outdated record deal. To this day, I blame my failure on the outfit I sported the night I showcased for Columbia Records. I should *never* have worn that ugly yellow-and-white polka-dot golf cap.

Another close call was when I met Phil Collins, who was standing behind me in the customs line at Boston's Logan International Airport. He looks exactly the same in real life. We chatted for a while about music and he was lovely. He asked me if I had any of my songs covered by other artists:

"Yes, actually!" I said. "One by a Canadian band."

Thing is, I didn't have any CDs in my purse. Can you believe it? (Always carry a CD in your purse!)

He was very good about it, however, and told me to just mail him a copy at: "Phil Collins, Geneva."

He said the post office knew him. Funny, I didn't believe him, so I never sent one. Perhaps I should rethink that.

Managers

THERE IS A PIVOTAL MOMENT in a songwriter's career and that is when a manager comes knock, knock, knockin' at your door.

Now, you may think the manager is going to be your lucky break: that somehow your manager is going to clear all the hurdles that have tripped you up in your career and deliver you to some great height of success.

He might. But just as likely he'll take advantage of you or start showing up in a bathing suit to your hot-yoga classes.

Truth is, managers have never much helped my career. I've gotten more done when I worked on my own.

From the start, I never put much stock in managers. I always thought of them as the sweaty guys who collected the money at the end of the night, or the ones who went golfing on weekends with record label executives, schmoozing their way to deals. "You should sign my artist!" he says as he drives a ball into the lake.

But maybe you'll be lucky and one day get the chance to work with a really great manager, someone who knows the business, and who has a huge amount of success under his belt. I got lucky once: Ron Fierstein from New York City, the guy I mentioned in the last chapter.

Ron had managed the careers of some of my own songwriting heroes: Shawn Colvin, Suzanne Vega, Mary Chapin Carpenter, and Dar Williams. He also happens to be the brother of comedic actor Harvey Fierstein.

How did I meet him? I used to get emails from an essayist named Bob Lefsetz. One time he wrote an article on Shawn Colvin. I had just released my first album, The Great Disappearing Act, and was exploring every avenue I could to get it out there. When you're an independent songwriter, you do everything in your power to promote your music.

I emailed Bob to congratulate him on his article. I also sent him my CD, and asked if he knew any managers who could help my career. Bob was gracious and put me in touch with Ron Fierstein. I sent Ron a copy of the album and we spoke over the phone soon after.

"I love your album," Ron said, "and so does everyone in my office. I'd like to come check out one of your shows. Can you tell me where you'll be playing in the next month?" He would not tell me which show he was coming to because he didn't want to make me "nervous."

Nervous? I was beside myself. I tried to get him to come to my Toronto show that week at C'est What: "They make a great falafel!" My hope was he would come to my own hometown where I'd be most comfortable. But Ron wasn't coming to a show in Toronto.

I looked for him everywhere I played. A couple weeks later, I was performing in Buffalo along with my friends Alex Wong and Devon Copley from the Brooklyn duo the Animators. After the show, a burly man with a moustache and big curly brown hair introduced himself. He looked like Gabe Kotter from Welcome Back, Kotter, wearing my Cher wig.

"I'd like to buy a CD," he said.

"Sure," I said, and sold him a copy.

"I'd like to buy another one," he said.

When he asked for a third CD, I realized he was teasing me. He handed me his business card instead of cash. Ron Fierstein.

Ron asked if I would sit at the back of the bar with him to talk business.

"We're interested in signing a three-year management contract with you," he said. "We'd like to fly you down to New York for some showcases. Does that sound good?"

It was better than good. I was in disbelief.

"And if you need any references, I would be happy to get you some," Ron said.

"That's okay," I said, knowing he was a famous manager. "Or, maybe one."

He chuckled again.

Afterwards, I called my auntie Carol from a payphone: "A big-time manager just flew up here from New York City! He actually took a *plane* and flew here to see my show! They want to sign me to a management deal! Can you believe it? This is a dream come true! I'm telling you, this is going to be my lucky break!"

"Well, you know," Auntie Carol said, "it took ten years for Kenny Rogers to become famous." She always used Kenny Rogers's career to encourage me.

That spring, Ron flew me to New York just as he'd promised. Not only that, he had a limousine waiting to greet me at the airport. That made me feel special. I sat in the back seat and was beaming at my good fortune when suddenly the limo driver crashed into another car on the way out of the airport parking lot. I had whiplash and had to ice my neck that whole night, before the show the next day.

Working in New York was a dream come true. I got to play all the hip bars in Manhattan, including the Bitter End, the Living Room, the Cutting Room, the Mercury Lounge, and the Bottom Line.

Over the next couple of years I went to New York to showcase in front of record labels like Columbia, Vanguard, and Razor & Tie. I call these my golden years because, truly, it was a great time in my life. I was working hard at music, and playing hard, too, spending after hours with musicians and musical theatre friends, running around New York City going to parties and dinners, starting conga lines in bars, and crashing on sofas in Brooklyn.

One night, three of us ran through an opened fire hydrant, just like in the movies. After that we ended up at a salsa bar. Some guy wearing a black hat who was a *really* good salsa dancer flung me across the dance floor. As we danced closer, he pressed his hand into my lower back, touching my sacrum ever so gently and sending a ripple right up my neck and into my head. I could have sworn he released twenty years of back pain right there. He was the best salsa dancer I'd ever seen.

I remember strolling through Central Park when the pink cherry blossoms were in full bloom, thinking how thrilling it was to be working as an artist in New York, a place that had captivated me since childhood, the city where people have always gone to make it in showbiz.

As far as managers go, Ron was one of the best guys around. He always treated me with kindness and respect. In the three years I worked with him, he never took a dime from me. He used to take me out for beautiful dinners around New York and introduce me to key people in the music industry.

The truth is, I never felt I measured up to the stature of Ron's other clients. He gave me so many incredible opportunities to play, yet I never felt like a real star. I was still young and had a long way to go as a performer.

I worked hard for a couple of years, shuffling back and forth from Toronto to New York, also playing shows in Ontario and other towns and cities on the east coast of America. Despite this, and even though Ron had every connection in the business, nobody would sign me. Ron had made the careers of Suzanne Vega and Shawn Colvin back in the day but with the shift to digital and downloads, the music industry was changing. No one was signing new artists.

Eventually, Ron retired from the business and wrote a novel. I've kept going, writing songs, making albums, and promoting them as best as I can.

Hits

THEY'RE ALWAYS LOOKING for hits in the music industry. Hits are songs you find yourself singing in the shower the day after you've heard them. Sometimes they're so insidious, they make you shake your head and slap your ears to get them out of your mind.

Hits are simple, catchy, clever songs that are typically three to four minutes in length, with the exception of "Free Bird." That song goes on forever.

If you don't have hits, managers and record labels will turn away from you, or else they'll throw you out their office window. "Now that's a hit!" they'll say. Or, "Sorry, no hits."

Sometimes you won't understand the lyrics to a hit song, even while singing it over and over. For example, "Sweet Dreams," by Annie Lennox never made any sense to me but the lyrics sound good and the rhymes are solid. Or what about "Relax," by Frankie Goes To Hollywood?" I only recently figured out that it's about having sex..

A hit song usually contains a hook, which is the part of the song that is particularly catchy and memorable, and which makes it even more difficult to stop singing. A hook can be sung by hordes of people in a pub as they stomp their feet and clink their beer glasses. Hooks bring people together. In "Hey Jude," everyone will lustily sing the "na-na-na-naa" part. Enemies will turn into friends during that part. Nations at war will lay down their arms and hold hands to sing, "Na-na-na-naaa" together. Hooks can be used as peacekeeping tactics.

At rock concerts people will flick their Bics or hold up their lit cell phones when the band plays a hit. It's a sign of great respect and connects everyone in the venue: adults, children, and the guys smoking weed in the rafters.

Hits can move you in sudden, unexpected ways. "Open Arms" by Journey makes me want to clutch a stranger, slow dance with him, grab his face, and make out with him.

Hits can literally hit us in the heart. When I hear "Both Sides Now," it's like a tap's been turned on. "Dust in the Wind" can put me in a fetal position for days.

Hits become the anthems of our lives. They contain universal messages that we can apply to our own experiences. If you're mad at your boyfriend, you can sing to him: "You're So Vain." You can always serenade a friend in need with "You've Got a Friend." Or, if you're having a particularly rough day, just put on "Stayin' Alive," and the Bee Gees will get you through it.

These days, the industry puts out hits that aren't very good. How Pharrell Williams's song "Happy" became a worldwide hit escapes me. It has no melody! In fact, "Happy" does not make me very happy at all! You can watch all kinds of people all over the world dancing to this song and being *happy*, but it just leaves me depressed and anxious every time I hear it!

Songwriters will always try to write hits because that's where the money is. But when you set out to write a hit, it doesn't work. It has to come from a genuine place. You can't force a hit, I don't think. You can't say: "Okay, today I'm going to write a hit." Unless you're Carole King and Gerry Goffin, who churned them out in a factory.

The best thing about hits for me, personally, is that when your parents call you to remind you that you do not have a day job, and ask what you're doing with your time, all you have to say is, "I'm actually writing a *hit* song," and they'll back right off and leave you alone for a couple of days.

Annabel

TURNS OUT I HAVE a hit song. Although it's a folk song. Does that count?

I wrote it for my beautiful grandmother who passed away in 1997. It knew it had to be special so I came up with a fingerpicking ballad. I tried to fashion it after some of my favourite Dylan tunes, like "Boots of Spanish Leather" and "Girl from the North Country." Once I had the melody, I set about writing lyrics, trying to be precise, and it took me three months. I called it "Annabel," after my grandmother whose name was Anne.

Annabel, Annabel, where did you go?
I've looked high and I've looked low
I've looked low and I've looked high
Tell me where does the spirit go when you die?
Where does the spirit go when you die?

After that, I toted around tapes of "Annabel" for a couple of years. I played it live at shows and on open stages. People always loved it. Many were moved to tears. Then I gave the tape to a music fan in Toronto who then gave it to the Duhks, who emailed: "Just to let you know, we've recorded 'Annabel' on our new album!"

I will always be grateful for the Duhks' hard touring schedule. "Annabel" reached so many people. Once at a yoga ashram, I met a very nice fellow from Louisiana who had heard the Duhks sing "Annabel" at a folk festival down South. It was one of those small-world feelings.

It didn't stop there. There were all kinds of people covering "Annabel" on YouTube. I even got a message from a guy in London who was in famous punk bands, The Members and The Vibrators. He had heard "Annabel" in the TV series *Hell on Wheels*. It used my song in the background of a steamy love scene. Can you imagine my shock watching those two naked bodies roll around to an innocent folk song about my grandmother?

The guy from the punk bands congratulated me on my songwriting and it started a lovely friendship between us.

I've seen pictures of the lyrics to "Annabel" tattooed on people's bodies. You know you have a hit song when people commit it to ink. I've also met several people who named their daughters Annabel because the song held so much meaning for them.

Sometimes I think my grandmother must be smiling down on me from heaven, pleased with the success of her song. Although she probably grimaces at the royalty cheques, which amount to about $400 a year.

Covers

PERFORMING COVER SONGS is a great way to strengthen your chops. It's also a great way to get inside the mind of the songwriter whose song you are covering. It can help you learn about the lyrical and musical choices they made in their writing, and it might even inspire you to write a song of your own.

The challenge in a cover is not to copy the original performance of the song but to make it your own, adding embellishments, like a distant pennywhistle. This can take time and work but it's often worthwhile.

But if you are planning to cover a song, for the love of god . . .

Don't play Bob Dylan's "Knockin' on Heaven's Door"!

How many times do I have to hear that wretched chorus, the same three chords droning on and on while the crowd sheepishly follows along? Please. Spare us the agony! I mean, Dylan wrote some pretty songs. How about "Girl from the North Country" or "Don't Think Twice, It's All Right?"

One of the great moments for any songwriter is when one of her own songs is covered, as happened for me with "Annabel."

After the Duhks recorded it on their album, guess what? They got a Grammy nomination for that album. The Duhks started playing shows and festivals everywhere. This worked out very well for me, because all the while they were going around the world with my song, I got to stay at home on my sofa watching *Law & Order.*

Now you can see all kinds of people covering "Annabel" on YouTube. I have no idea who they are, and some of them do look a bit disheveled. I don't make a penny from their covers. Nonetheless, it is an honour! Of all the songs in the world, they chose to cover mine. I found a version of "Annabel" sung by a male choir called the Beelzebubs. They were from Tufts University in Boston. How they found my song I'll never know.

Years later, I had a second song covered by Dar Williams. My New York manager, Ron, had introduced us many years earlier. When Dar messaged me that she was going to record "Weight of the World," I thought I'd died and gone to heaven. Imagine, a song that took me fifteen minutes to write was bound for an album by one of the great singer-songwriters of our time, one of my own songwriting heroes. Her decision to cover "Weight of the World" was so affirming that for the first time in a while I thought all of my relatives—and the guests at that one Rosh Hashana brunch—might have been wrong that I was crazy for having the dream of making music. (You are not crazy for having the dream of making music.)

It truly is one of the great moments in a songwriter's life when another artist covers one of your songs. How it happens is still mysterious to me. Maybe it's luck. Maybe it's timing. Maybe someone has a good heart and shares your music with someone in a high position. I'm just as mystified as you are. But don't be surprised if one day you find a stranger in desperate need of a shave and a haircut singing one of your songs on YouTube.

Co-Writing

I WAS GOING THROUGH a dry spell when Ron called from New York:

"So, how's the writing going?" he asked.

"Oh, you know . . . Genius takes time!" I said.

Ron very graciously set up a co-writing session for me with a producer he knew in Manhattan. I met the producer at his office in a high-rise on the thirtieth floor. There were framed gold records of famous female artists all over his walls. Not intimidating at all!

The producer went over to his upright piano and played a line of something he'd come up with. Then I went over to the piano and played a line of something I'd come up with.

And then? Nothing.

A whole hour went by. You could hear crickets. I twiddled my thumbs and whistled.

We sat there looking at each other, smiling uncomfortably, and then parted with a warm handshake. The meeting was a total flop. I figured I was a failure at co-writing and I haven't tried it since.

It's just that it felt so unnatural! I mean, can you imagine walking into a room with a complete stranger and writing a deep, intimate song together? You might as well get naked and launch into full-contact improvisational/authentic movement dance. Why not invite a total stranger into your therapy session and let him listen as you spill your guts?

Thing is, writing a song, for me, is deeply personal. It usually happens when I'm going through something intense and need to speak about it from the heart. Not in an office tower surrounded by other people's gold records.

It also feels strange to share the rights to those confessions with someone I don't know. What I mean by "share the rights to those confessions," is that you have to decide on how to split the percentage of what you contributed to the song. You can see how the situation can get ugly. "I had my heart ripped out for this song and you want 50 percent?"

Not only that, what happens if you don't like what your partner writes? What if they write something cheesy? How do you tell them you don't like what they've written? Would you be polite, maybe lie to them, say something like, "Oh yeah! That's, like, *really* deep, man, and I think we should use it," when you actually want to throw up?

What happens if you *do* tell the truth: "You know what, man? That idea *sucks* and I hate it!"

Then your co-writer says, "Well, you know what? I think your *face* really sucks!"

And then you're swinging guitars at each other's shins.

"Don't you know I've had three hits in Nashville?"

"You call those *hits*?"

A friend of mine says there's something inherently inauthentic about co-writing. He would feel like a prostitute sitting with three guys at a table, writing songs for a publishing company. He says you can't mechanically churn out songs just to get a cut on someone's album. I agree with him. Songs, for me, have to come from a real place.

I'm sure there are people out there skilled at writing on commercial terms. But if you're an artist willing to share the truth about your lived experience, maybe you should go that road alone. Or find someone you trust, someone with whom you really click.

I say that, yet the truth is, so many great songs come from co-writes. My two favourite pairs are Lennon and McCartney, despite the quibbles over who did what, and Elton John and Bernie Taupin. Talk about glorious collaborations. How did they do it? Séances? Mushrooms?

No harm, I guess, in giving it a try. Co-writing seems to give you cred these days. If you're really having a bad time, just slip out for a bathroom break and never return.

Anything Can Happen (The Bagel Store Disaster)

YOU NEVER KNOW WHERE your career might take you. Maybe to superstardom. Maybe to East Peoria. The one thing you can count on is that your career will take you somewhere you never expected to be. Mine took me to the emergency ward.

It was September 24, 2003. We were going into the studio in Toronto to record the follow-up to my first album, *The Great Disappearing Act*. The band was setting up. I figured I had time to get some bagels. Musicians always appreciate free food. For most of them, it's that or starve. And I needed bagels, too. That morning, I'd had a very large coffee. In Starbucks terms, a Venti, and I was jittery from not having eaten breakfast.

I was wearing a pair of baggy blue cotton harem pants and a white T-shirt that was splattered in multicoloured paint. The T-shirt, very Jackson Pollock, made me feel like an artist. My hair was to my shoulders and I was wearing a new pair of blue-framed glasses. To top it all off, I threw on a pair of white flip-flops, since the sun was out and it was still a warm day, even though it was already late September. Before leaving my apartment, I had checked myself out in my full-length mirror. I still hadn't found my look but I felt good in my vibe. Plus, you always want to be comfortable in the studio.

I'll never forget that image in the mirror. It was as if I was recognizing myself for the first time as a strong, whole, grounded being. I was thirty-three years old. The coming week, I was moving to New York to work more closely with my manager. I had already sublet a place in Brooklyn.

I was buzzing with excitement on my way to the bagel shop. It was one of those rare moments in a songwriter's life where your serotonin levels are soaring and you feel like things might finally be going your way.

There I was, putting bagels into a paper bag. Two plain. Two rye. Two pumpernickel. And it happened.

There was a huge explosion. It sounded like a bomb going off. I felt a gust of wind at the back of my neck. My body was pushed towards the back wall of the little shop. I felt the most excruciating pain in my arms and legs.

My mind raced to make sense of what was going on. I couldn't move. My legs were pinned under metal bagel racks. There was heavy dust in the air and shattered glass everywhere. I turned my head and saw a car in the middle of the store.

"Help!" I said, when I finally found my words. "Somebody help me!"

A muscular guy came over and tried dislodge my arms and legs from all the metal. My right shin was twisted up towards my pelvis in a way that wasn't normal. I had a vision of myself in a wheelchair for the rest of my life. I heard a voice in my head: "At least, I'll still have my singing voice." I still wasn't sure what had happened but I was already making a deal with the devil.

"The ambulance is coming," somebody shouted. "Just don't move."

I yelled to the woman at the counter: "Can you please make me a bagel with cream cheese to go? I'm starving. I didn't have any breakfast!"

No one believes I said that as I lay there crushed, waiting on an ambulance, but I did. And they wouldn't give me food. Some onlooker said I shouldn't eat anything before I got to the hospital.

First came the fire trucks, then the ambulance. I had to brush away shards of glass that were cutting my skin before they got me onto the stretcher. By then, I was going on adrenalin. My body was in acute pain but my mind was hyper-alert. When they got me into the back of the ambulance, I blurted to one of the emergency technicians: "My father is a doctor at Sunnybrook Hospital," and I recited his number. "Can you please call him?"

I was about to pass out when I remembered I had something in my purse. "And this is my CD," I said, holding it up from the stretcher. "I'm a songwriter. If you know anyone that can help my career, can you please play it for them?"

"I'm sorry, hon," one of the EMT guys said. "We're not allowed to take gifts on the job. Just hang on, sweetie, we're almost there. We're taking you to Sunnybrook." That's when I passed out for good.

When I came around, I was lying in Sunnybrook Emergency and my father's clear blue eyes were looking down at me. His face was expressionless. Surgeons are like that.

"I'm okay, Dad. Are you okay?" I said. I started to tell him what had happened but they quickly wheeled me into a room where they cut off my harem pants and lovely Jackson Pollock T-shirt in order to examine me. After a full day of tests, they discovered the only thing broken, miraculously, was my leg. I had surgery the next day.

Word spread fast. It seems everyone in Toronto found out about my accident. It was in the local newspaper. The local evening news showed me being carried away on the stretcher. Every time I took a taxi—I was on crutches for three months—I would explain to the driver what had happened to me and hear: "That was *you* in the bagel store?"

"Make plans and god laughs," my father said. I never made it to my recording session and I never made it to New York. I spent the next year in rehab, learning how to walk again, and trying to regain my strength. Not surprisingly, the guys in the studio that day expected me to pay for the missed session. Once out of the hospital, I had to visit them separately (while still on my crutches) to pay them for their time. Musicians need to get paid, even if you missed the session because you were crushed in a bagel store. Getting them bagels.

The name of the shop was What A Bagel. For years, I endured quips like: "What a bagel that was!" and "You could have been toast!" The *worst* was when I'd get up onstage and people would yell, "Break a leg!" since I really did break my leg, and I can tell you, it's nothing to sneeze at.

When you survive a near-death incident, people come out of the woodwork. I received cards, stuffed animals, boxes of chocolates, fruit baskets, fruit *dipped* in chocolate, phone calls from far away, and I had some wonderful and meaningful visits with friends and family. People I hardly knew came into my life at that time, and it made me realize I am loved, and that I had no choice but to let that in.

Despite this, I was deeply depressed. As far as I was concerned, my life was over. Instead of the sublet in Brooklyn, I had moved into my parents' house because I needed their help. Sometimes I would lie in their backyard at night, weeping. "Why did this happen to me?" It was a question that would obsess me for a long time to come.

Something about getting crushed in a bagel bakery inclines you to seek spiritual guidance. Altogether, I saw two rabbis, a priest, and a shaman, but I'll focus on the rabbis.

The first rabbi, a Reform man, came to see me while I was still in the hospital. I was sitting in bed with a morphine drip in my arm. "Rabbi," I asked him, "why did this happen to me?"

"Bad things happen to people all over the world," he said. "You are not so special."

It wasn't what I wanted to hear at that moment. I was so angry, I wanted to throw one of my stuffed animals at him. But I thought about it some more. It was true. For most of my life, I had felt immune to terrible phenomena. Death by tsunami, or earthquake. Famine. Having a piano fall on my head. Bagel store disasters. Those were things that happened to other people.

One night I shot up in bed in a panic. The rabbi was right! I'm not so special. I'm going to die like everyone else! I may have escaped this time but one day it's really going to happen. I was so upset I had to eat an entire box of marshmallow Viva Puffs cookies before I could fall back asleep.

Contests and Competitions

THERE IS A LOT OF COMPETITION in the music business so be prepared to compete. For instance, you might want to enter your songs in a songwriting contest.

I sometimes wonder, what is the point of entering a contest. Maybe it is so you can win a not-real-gold medal to wear around your neck or, at the very least, a pair of Bose speakers. But let's face it, deep down inside, what you're really hoping for is that the Rolling Stones will ask you to tour with them, or your new album will become a worldwide *hit*, or they'll use one of your videos in an iPhone commercial, or something like that.

So far I've won three songwriting competitions, all of them out of Nashville. That makes it sound very fancy and all: "Nashville," as if I've done something special. But to tell you the truth, I wasn't the only winner. In fact, there were so many winners—dozens upon dozens—that they had to call us "finalists." But what were we, then? Finalists or winners? I mean, finalist is not the same as winner, right? If we're all just finalists, aren't we all losers, too? I thought about this for some time and decided that finalist was at least better than honourable mention, or dishonourable mention.

Finalist, or winner, it's good to enter your music in competitions. You never know what's going to happen.

For example, one time I was invited to enter a talent contest at a theatre in Toronto. It wasn't a bad gig. They had a steak-and-peas dinner on the menu before the show. Performers ate for free.

That night there were dancers and musicians, magicians, and even some circus people on the bill. Turns out, I won that contest, too. Except so did the magician, the dancer, the fire-breather, the fortune-teller, the blues guy on guitar, and even the circus people. In fact, all the "talent" that night were winners, and the way they let us know was by playing madly on a triangle by the side of the stage.

At the very end of the evening, they made us all stand in a line and sing: "We are the worrrrrrld / We are the children / We are the ones who make a brighter day, so let's start givinnnnn." I mean, you couldn't back out of it! What were you supposed to do when they called your name to get back up there? Sneak out the backstage exit? It was a famine-relief anthem!

Well, after all that, they didn't give us prizes. Not so much as a toaster or a free movie pass. Not even a new pair of handcuffs for the magician. In fact, I can't even remember where the money went that night but I did get a free steak-and-peas dinner out of it.

Another competition in which I became "finalist" instead of "winner" was in the grade six spelling bee. I *almost* made it to the end, until they gave me "sandwich," and I forgot to add the *d*. Can you imagine? I was devastated! I still think about it to this day. The worst thing is, I *still* can't spell that word! Thank god for autocorrect.

The only good thing about music industry competitions is the odd free meal. That, and they drive you to work harder. Competition might be what gets your next album to the finish line. So pick up that microphone stand, loosen up with a couple of kicks and lunges (be mindful of your knees), and fight to make the best music you can, even though thousands of other songwriters around the world will do the same. Do your best, and you always win.

Song-in-the-Round

I WANT TO KNOW WHO invented the song-in-the-round. Whose idea was it to have four songwriters sitting on a stage, like ducks in a row, taking turns with their songs? Do you have any idea how long you have to wait before your turn comes around again? Centuries!

You play your song, get all warmed up, your vocal cords primed, then you have to shut the hell up for half an hour, or more, until the other three songwriters play *their* songs, by which time you need to warm up all over again.

What are you supposed to do sitting there for that long? I guess you could stare at a point on the wall. You could begin to count: "One thousand, two, one thousand . . . " but since the audience is watching, you'll have to smile, and pretend that you're really enjoying yourself up there, but really you're morbidly depressed, and your back is killing you from having to sit there for so long and wait for your turn to come around again!

Not only that, but what happens if you don't like the songs the other performers are playing? You'll have to nod your head in time, as if you're really digging their music. But actually you're thinking: When in *god's* name can I get off this stage?

Once I ordered a ribs dinner and ate it while waiting my turn in a song-in-the-round. Then I enjoyed a nice glass of red wine, followed by a cigarette. As a matter of fact, by the time it was my turn to play again, I'd had dessert, too. And there was still time to floss my teeth!

And what about the audience? Do you think *they're* having a good time when we sing songs-in-the-round? What if there's only one musician they came to see? They have to sit through all the performers they've never even heard of to get the next song of the musician they like. By the time the show is over they're lucky to have heard three songs by their favourite.

Do club bookers realize how tedious the format is? They use it all the time, especially at folk festivals. I guess they think it's a way to kill four folkie birds with one stone but which one of those songwriters is really having a good time up there? I mean, let's face it, who wants to take turns? Wouldn't you want to have your own show instead?

The worst is when you finally get to play your song and someone in the song-in-the-round starts jamming with you. Who gave them permission? Suddenly, they're ruining your song with the wrong harmony, or banging uncontrollably on a cowbell or something like that. It's preposterous!

Music Conferences

FOLK MUSIC CONFERENCES ARE where rumpled songwriters from all over the country roam freely in hotel rooms and lobbies, lounge around on sofas and fingerpick John Prine tunes. A music conference can be a great place to meet other songwriters, book gigs with each other, and make lasting connections. But if you think a conference is going to promote your career, forget it.

You can bring all kinds of promotional materials: CDs, buttons, stickers, one-sheets, pens, rolls of toilet paper with your face on them. You can drop all this stuff into bins at the registration table hoping to god some festival director will look at it. But waiting for miracles is a waste of time, and wouldn't you rather be smoking doobies on a balcony with a country producer from Nashville?

One time I chased down a high-profile promoter in the hallway of an Ottawa music conference. "Hi, I'm Kat Goldman," I said. "Would you have the time to sit and talk with me about my career?"

The promoter gave me ten minutes before he went to speak on a panel. "You have to know what you want," he said. Like that was supposed to help. It's the same thing every industry person said. I swear they rehearse it, "What is it you *want*?"

"For Christ's sake," I should have answered, "what do you think I want? I want my new album to be number one across the world! I want to win a Grammy for album of the year! I want my song playing in every goddamn elevator till the end of time! Now can you please pass my music on to some-body who can help me? 'Cause I'm drowning here!"

If you're going to spend big bucks to attend a folk music conference, know the only reason you're going is to smoke on a balcony and make some new friends. But don't think it's going to help your career. And don't expect to get any sleep. Those nut bars are going to play banjos all night. In the hallways, the lobby, the elevators, and in your room.

How to Schmooze

I F YOU'RE GOING TO WORK in the music industry, you might want to learn how to schmooze. What does it mean to schmooze? Dictionary. com says:

> *verb (used without object),* **schmoozed, schmooz·ing.**
> 1. to chat idly; gossip.
> *noun*
> 2. idle conversation; chatter.

In the music industry, schmoozing means talking up people to take an interest in you or your artist. I know a bunch of high-profile managers in Toronto. They would all get together to play poker at one of their houses. The biggest manager there apparently played in his socks and had smelly feet, although no one said a word about it. His artist was the most famous person in the room.

I can picture them all sitting there, holding up their cards, and one manager says: "My artist is catching a buzz right now. You have to listen to his album! It's gonna be *huge*." Next thing you know, the artist is catching a buzz, then he's huge.

Of course, some schmoozers are better than others. I've found the best ones to be on the business side of things, not the artists themselves. That's the thing about schmoozing—it seldom works when you do it on your own behalf. Nobody likes a songwriter tooting her own horn, walking up to some bigwig at a party saying, "You should listen to my album *The Workingman's Blues*! It's really catching a buzz right now. It's going to be *big*, man. *Exclaim!* magazine said it was 'lyrically ambitious'!" They'd probably just roll their eyes and reach for another hors d'oeuvre.

The more I think about it, I really don't think it flies to schmooze on your own behalf. I was never comfortable with it, myself. The idea is to get a team of people around you who will sing your praises. Get someone *else* to do the dirty work, pushing your music onto others who can do something with it.

This is where having a big-time manager can come in handy. At one point, Ron was talking to Vanguard, Columbia, and Razor & Tie. All I had to do was write music, play shows, and try to find the right outfit to wear.

It is a rare songwriter who takes it upon himself to be a schmoozer. Jesse B used to be all over town. He had platinum-blond hair and a cute face. He made some headway with his career in the early 2000s. First time I met him was at a Halloween party where we were introduced by Peaches, who was dressed as Ralph Macchio in *The Karate Kid*.

Next time I saw Jimmy he was butting in line, right in front of me, to talk to the frontman of a band that was playing in the city. "Jesse?" I said. "It's Kat. Kat Goldman. Remember we met at that Halloween party where Peaches was dressed as the Karate Kid?"

Jesse didn't remember me. He was too busy trying to get to the front of the line.

No matter how many times I bumped into Jesse, he'd always look baffled, trying to place me from somewhere. One time I saw him at the crosswalk at the corner of Queen and Spadina. "Jesse," I said, "It's Kat. Kat Goldman. Remember, we met at that Halloween party where Peaches was dressed as the Karate Kid?" Nothing.

Leaving aside his terrible memory, Jesse was a dedicated schmoozer. One time he got an opening spot for Aimee Mann. I caught glimpses of him and his blond hair backstage. He was stuffing his face with pizza before the show, gloating that he got the opening spot.

I've heard nothing of his career lately. Maybe the schmooze police caught up to him.

Is there a point to schmoozing? Does all the hype and talk matter in the end? Maybe. It seems to me that the people I know who caught breaks in this business benefitted from luck or timing, and others who opened doors for them.

There are always rumours of people paying to have others play their music. In the radio business, it's known as "payola." Announcers are bribed to give airplay to a musician. But after the huge expense of making your album and slapping your come-hither posters all over town, who has money to pay people off?

Nowadays, I use sex appeal to get what I want. When I released my video for "Release Me" on YouTube, I had three voluptuous backup dancers in tight hot-pink dresses. I was up front doing some of my best choreography in a tight black top that showed off my cleavage. I figure, who needs to schmooze? Actions speak louder than words.

Co-Bills

ONCE IN A WHILE YOU may be asked to perform with another songwriter. You will be co-bills. I once had a famous male co-bill who wanted to get me in the sack. Not that there's anything wrong with that. Yours, in fact, might be an offer you can't refuse.

While I've had some lovely male co-bills over the years, there was one guy I met when I was still young, just starting out, who . . . let's just say he wasn't my type. Boy, was I stupid. Just because he'd hung out with Bob Dylan and Joni Mitchell back in the day, I took the bait and agreed to join him at the bar for a glass of wine after our show.

"I really dig that song you played, 'The Underground.' You're a real-deal songwriter," he said.

"Oh, thanks," I said. I blushed and took another sip of wine.

"Songwriters aren't treated very well, you know," he said. "This is a tough business."

The more he talked, the more I sipped my wine. Little did I know, Shirley, a tough lawyer and songwriter well-known in the music scene, was watching the whole scene from the other end of the bar. She'd also been drinking.

"C'mere!" she said, waving at me.

I walked to the other end of the bar where Shirley swung her arm around my neck and pulled my ear against her mouth. "Heeesh a creep!" she said, "Don't go home with him. I'm ordering you a cab."

Next thing I knew, she whipped me into a taxi after I'd said a quick goodnight to my co-bill, whose last words were: "Can I get your number?" Of course, I gave it to him.

The following day I got a call. "It's your co-bill," he said. "Would you like to go out for dinner tonight?"

"Sure," I told him. "I'll pick you up." I really thought it would just be dinner and an opportunity to plug my music. Like I said, stupid.

We met at his hotel. When I got to the lobby, the first thing he said to me was: "I'm not feeling that well, baby. Do you want to go back to my room and order a pizza?"

Pizza! The red flags were waving vigorously. I had this really bad feeling come over me. What can I say? I hadn't seen it coming. Luckily, I had enough wits about me to clue in now; I rejected his offer and steered him to dinner in the hotel restaurant. Boy, did he look annoyed. Back in the day, he must have had any chick he wanted. He just sat there looking bored to tears as I ate my fettuccine alfredo. I bet he couldn't wait to say, "Check!" to the waitress.

On my way out, I gave him a copy of my first CD, although I'm sure it ended up in the hotel trash. I went home feeling foolish. But the next day, I picked myself up and called him.

"Hi!" I said. "It's your co-bill. Do you remember when you said I was a real-deal songwriter?"

"Yeah," he answered.

"Well, I was just wondering if I could use that as a quote for my music."

There was a pause. "Use it for everything it's got, baby," he said.

So I did.

Sometimes Try
a New City

AFTER MY GREAT BAGEL DISASTER and my conversation with the Reform rabbi, I was tortured by a new awareness of my mortality. I also developed an acute case of post-traumatic stress disorder. Every time I turned on my computer, I thought it was going to explode. I feared poisonous gas was seeping from my heating vents. The insurance guy sent me a couple of social workers, but they weren't very helpful. How was anybody who hadn't been felled by a freak accident in a bagel store going to understand what I was going through? The insurer should have sent someone who had been struck by lightning. It was a lonely time.

I decided to speak to an Orthodox rabbi. Rabbi Number Two took me for lunch at a kosher deli. It was nice of him but I couldn't take my eyes of the glass at the front of the restaurant. As we were leaving, I asked my question: "Rabbi, why did this happen to me?"

"It's over now," he answered. "You have to move forward."

So simple. He was right, too. I had been given a second chance at life. It was up to me what I did with it. I began to write out a bucket list. These were my top five goals:

1. Go back to school to finish my bachelor's degree.
2. Get married in my bare feet on a beach in Mexico.

3.   Retire to a beach in Mexico.
4.   Learn Spanish.
5.   Make more albums.

Over time, I went from two crutches to one crutch to a cane. The cane was sexy, and sometimes a kind gentleman would hold the door for me at a café. But even though my bones started to heal and I had learned how to walk again, my mental state was getting worse. Every day, I'd break down into epic sobbing fits. I couldn't listen to music, except for John Lennon's greatest-hits album. Songs like "Instant Karma!" and "Watching the Wheels" had cosmic messages that comforted me. I couldn't play my own material, except for one song which, ironically, I'd written a year before my accident: it was called "Weight of the World." I would sing and strum it on a tiny guitar a friend lent me during my recovery.

> *You want to take it off*
> *It's the weight of the world*
> *You want to set it free*
> *Just for today,*
> *Can't always be the one*
> *To heal everything*
> *And the weight of the world*
> *Was never yours to keep.*

Mostly I was exhausted. By seven at night, I'd be lying on my sofa, watching crime shows to numb myself. And that was sort of how my mid-thirties went. I kept writing songs but I didn't go out much to hear or play music. My body was too tired. I rode the waves of various depressions while everyone else I knew was getting married, having kids, or getting promoted in their jobs.

In 2007, four years after the accident, I did manage to record my second album, *Sing Your Song*. I had my release concert at the Rivoli in Toronto with a four-piece string orchestra. The house was packed, mostly with friends and family. It was the start of a comeback. CBC Radio named *Sing Your Song* one of the top albums of 2007. When I sent a copy to Dar Willliams, she wrote: "I can't imagine the world without it." She later covered "Weight of the World" on her album *Emerald*.

I did various *Sing Your Song* tour loops from Toronto to Boston to New York City, and sometimes to Ottawa and Montreal. I'd frequent the annual Campfire Festival at the famed folk venue Club Passim in Harvard Square, where songwriters would come from all over North America to play songs-in the-round and meet and hear each other. Sometimes we'd all just sit cross-legged in the red-brick alleyway outside the club and play songs. That's where I saw Regina Spektor for the first time. She had a look, and the confidence to go with, *and* she was a piano prodigy, three things I lacked in my own career. Not long after that, she broke into a bigger market. I listened to her albums for inspiration.

Another time I met Norah Jones outside the Living Room in Manhattan, where I also played shows for a number of years. I told her how much I liked her album. She was so friendly and down-to-earth. I did shows in Wakefield, Quebec, at a hip venue called the Black Sheep Inn where the musicians were boarded upstairs in supposedly haunted rooms. CBC did a live recording of one of my shows there. I toured Western Canada and had a few dates in France.

But in 2008, at age thirty-nine, I had another breakdown. I wasn't moving on from the accident. I just couldn't see my future. My mother always said, "If you're unhappy with your life, change it."

At some point, you, too, will get fed up with where you are with your life in music. You might decide to do what I did. In June 2009, I packed up my car with a bag of summer clothes, my guitar, my keyboard, my dog, and a vacuum cleaner, and headed for Boston.

Technicalities

I F YOU'RE GOING TO BE A singer-songwriter working in the music industry, there are some technical things that you will need to know. You will need to know about patch cords, and soundboards, and microphones, and sound monitors, and DI boxes, and, to tell you the truth, to this day, I still do not know whether you stick the patch cord into the input or the output of the DI box. And what in god's name does "DI" even stand for?

I admit there have been times when I wish I'd had more technical finesse than I possess. One time I did a concert in a big, beautiful church, a three-hundred seater, as they say. When I finished my set, the audience applauded. I said "thank-you," and did a perfectly polite little curtsy, and turned around to walk off to the wings.

Except I forgot to unplug my guitar! This brought me to an abrupt stop halfway across the stage. The patch cord whipped my body around to face my audience again. I smiled apologetically, unplugged my guitar, and tripped over various cables before finally making it offstage and swiftly exiting the building.

Way back in the day, during my very first shows, I used to take an inordinately long to time to tune my guitar. I used to do it by ear, you know, the way Paul Simon did in those early live recordings of Simon and Garfunkel.

Sometimes my tuning would go on for fifteen minutes! I sort of thought it was cute. But my parents, at their front-row table, would roll their eyes and noisily stir their Manhattans. It took me *years* to realize that you could buy guitar tuners that make the job much easier and take the guesswork out of it.

For many years, I used to take extra time onstage at the end of my show, coiling up the patch cord real slow between my elbow and my thumb, while peering out into the audience. I did this to show just how *experienced* I was with musical technology, the real pro kind of stuff.

Did you know that if you loop one end of a patch cord and whirl it around in the air over your head, you can use it like a lasso? This gets the crowd uproarious.

Once I played in a venue so tiny you could use it to store spices. In the middle of my set, the promoters set off a dry-ice machine. They seemed to have mistaken our gig for a Mötley Crüe concert. Well, with that room so small, the fog started to spread all around me during one of my more "serious" guitar ballads. I could barely see anything in front of me, let alone breathe! There was nothing but white smoke. After that, I said I would never play in dry ice again.

Now, did you know that a microphone has a sweet spot? Rest assured, this doesn't mean you're supposed to lick it or stroke it fondly. What it means is that, depending on how you tilt your head, and where you direct your mouth, singing into that spot produces better sound.

Sometimes if you sing too close to your mic, your chin will knock it and make it bob up and down. When this happens to me, I just bob my head up and down in time to the bobbing microphone, as if I'm really getting into the music, and hope no one will notice it was a mistake.

Don't be afraid of the technical side of music. Just ask your soundperson, your engineer, your producer, or your band anything you still don't know. For example, which goddamn hole *is* it you put the patch cord into? How do you turn the violinist down when he's playing an unbearably loud Zeppelin riff over your mellow acoustic folk number? Or how do you cut the house music over the loudspeaker, so it isn't playing in the background during your show?

Whoops. Gotta go! My foot's caught in some other cable.

Be Prepared
to Improvise

YOU CAN NEVER PREDICT what's going to happen during your show, so be prepared to improvise. Take, for example, the time I played at the Living Room in New York City. I was really hammering it out on piano during one of my more "upbeat" numbers, when part of the instrument fell on my leg. Of course somebody was filming and it is now on YouTube.

The soundguy had to come up onstage to do repairs right in the middle of my song! So what I did was speak to the crowd to ease their discomfort, and I smiled despite my throbbing knee, as the sound guy fidgeted under my legs. Then I picked up right where I'd left off and sang the remainder of the song. It was just like nothing had happened.

Then there was the time I opened for Dar Williams in a quaint little theatre in Maine. I was sitting alone in the dressing room and noticed some chocolate chip cookies on a plate. I wondered if it would be okay to eat from the main act's rider.

Well, I only ate one cookie but within fifteen minutes I was having an anaphylactic reaction. My face blew up like Dory the fish. Never eat from the main act's rider!

Just then, Dar called me back up onstage to join her in her encore, "This Land Is Your Land." How could I say no? She was paying tribute to the late Pete Seeger. Except I didn't know all the words!

So what I did was, I pretended to be relaxed up there, like it was real easygoing and all, like I'd been singing that song my whole life. Then I sort of mumbled along while my mouth continued to swell:

"From the New York Fnaaaaa-Shaaaaaaaaaa . . . to the something islands . . ."

I tried my best to smile, swaying in time to the music with Dar and one other guest as my lips got bigger and bigger.

As soon as the song ended, I slipped out the doors of the theatre as fast as I could and made for the car, refusing to sign autographs from the exiting crowd (well, just one autograph). I drove three hours back to Boston where I was admitted to emergency and slept all night on a drip.

Another time I was late getting to a rock benefit concert, arriving right when the host announced my name over the loudspeaker:

"And now, Kat Goldmaannnnn!" he said, as I hurried towards the stage.

As I rushed on, I realized I didn't have my capo or thumb pick with me. I had to spill my entire purse there onstage in front of two hundred people. I was still crouching down, front and centre, with my back to the audience, going through lipsticks and throwing crumpled Kleenexes over my shoulder, when the host called out my name a second time, even as I was squatting at his feet:

"Ladies and gentlemen, here by popular request, all the way from Toronto, Canada"—he stalled—"let's give a warm round of applause for Kat Goldmaannnnnn!"

I finally found my capo and thumb pick, climbed my way back upright, clutching the microphone stand like a drunken pole dancer, and held my thumb pick high in the air:

"And for my next trick!" I said.

You never know when your gig will go south so be prepared to improvise. You might also take measures to dispel bad juju before going in front of the audience. I like to do a sage smudging ceremony in the dressing room, pounding my chest and chanting *om*. You might prefer a hit of Jack Daniel's. Whatever you do, don't forget your thumb pick, and just in case, bring your EpiPen.

Stage Fright

I T'S NATURAL TO BE NERVOUS before and/or during a show. So many performers get stage fright. I actually take it to be a good sign when I have nerves. You want to channel this energy into your performance. In fact, I get worried when I'm *not* nervous because it might indicate a lack of focus. One thing to realize is that unless you're playing to a bunch of skinheads, like I did in Syracuse, New York, one night, the audience, for the most part, is there for you. They want you to succeed.

There are lots of ways to deal with stage fright. First of all, don't focus on the schmuck yawning in the front row. Why focus on him? He's just going to psych you out. And anyhow, who knows? Maybe his wife just left him. Maybe your music is not his cup of tea. So what? If you see anyone who looks bored, look away. To do otherwise is self-sabotage. Focus instead on people who seem engaged in what you're doing. If you can't find any, pick a spot on the wall and stare at it.

Another way to cope with the jitters is to practise. The more you rehearse, the better equipped you'll be when it's time to perform. Your muscles will remember what to do should you have an out-of-body experience onstage.

Another technique is to close your eyes for a bit. Do you remember David Cassidy from *The Partridge Family*? He was always closing his eyes when he sang. I used to think it was a shtick. Then I tried it at one of my own shows and realized that closing your eyes gives you a break from the audience. It keeps you safe for a moment. It gives you the opportunity to collect yourself, centre yourself in what you're doing. And people will think you look cool like David Cassidy.

The idea is to come into the present moment. Any movement or relaxation exercises can be helpful before a show. A few minutes of stretching or cardio will also do the trick. There are all kinds of yoga-for-anxiety videos on YouTube. They show you how to shake out your body, roll soft balls against your chest (that didn't come out right), or stand on one foot for balance. Forward bends calm the nervous system. You can curl up in child pose and take long, deep breaths. Just be awake when they call you onstage.

Another way to stay present is to focus on the emotion behind what you're singing. Do you remember what you were feeling when you wrote the song? You want to conjure this experience onstage. And if you can't connect to the original emotion behind your lyrics, use whatever you're feeling that night to fuel the delivery of your song.

Don't forget, you have a special gift to share with the world. You might think of yourself as the host of your own party, the leader of the pack, the master of ceremonies, the conductor of the orchestra, the shaman who's going to transform the energy in the room. That stage belongs to you so don't be afraid to own it.

One last tactic: set an intention before you perform. It can be very specific. For instance, you could say to yourself, "Tonight I want people to connect with the words to my songs," or, "Tonight I will not trip on the sound monitor again." I find that if I set an intention, it helps to ground me.

You might also turn to drugs or alcohol, but I don't recommend it. In high school, we smoked a joint the size of a zucchini before one of our rock shows and when I went to sing at the microphone, I sounded like Alvin and the Chipmunks. Also, you don't want to forget your lyrics in the middle of the song.

Stage fright is a normal part of being a performer. Channel this energy into delivering a truly powerful show. And if all else fails, just picture the audience in their birthday suits. That works, doesn't it?

So You Made a Mistake

I'S THE MOMENT WE ALL DREAD: What happens if you make a mistake? Forget a lyric, miss a cue, play a wrong note.

Don't worry. There are several things you can do if you mistake in the middle of your performance. And believe me, I've tried them all.

1. Stop and say, "Oh God! I made a mistake. Now I've done it. I've screwed up! I'm so sorry. I do apologize. Sorry. No, really, I'm sorry!" Then you can offer your CDs at half price at the end of the night.

2. Sit there paralyzed, looking stunned as if you've just been tasered. Then, when you finally come around, get up from your chair and walk offstage, throw your hands in the air, and say, "That's it! I'm training in chair yoga."

3. In an instance when you've forgotten words to a song, ask if anyone in the audience knows your lyrics. That's when someone will pull out an iPhone and say, "Hang on . . . still downloading . . . almost got it . . . okay, it's . . ." Then you can invite them onstage to sing the rest of the song with you.

4. Stop and say, "Aww, forget it. You know what? Let's just try something else. Does everyone know 'Kumbaya'?"

5. Keep going! Don't worry about it! Most likely, people did not notice. And even if they did, the audience likes to be a part of those moments. Imperfection makes for a more interesting performance. People want to see your vulnerability. It gives them a great sense of relief to see that—after all—you, too, are human.

Drummer Jokes

ANOTHER THING YOU CAN DO when you've screwed up onstage and need to distract the audience is tell drummer jokes.

How do you know when the stage is level?
If the drool from the drummer is coming out on both sides.

Not great, I know, but let's see you come up with better. And don't give me the ones we've all heard before:

What's the difference between a drummer and a large pizza?
A Large pizza can feed a family of four.

Or . . .

What's the last thing the drummer said to his band?
Let's try one of my songs.

For songwriters who've spent years strumming their lonely acoustic instruments in coffee houses, playing with a drummer for the first time can be exciting. It can really take your songs up a notch. It might even make you want to throw away your own instrument and start dancing in the middle of the rehearsal room.

Over time, you'll familiarize yourself with the different parts of a drum set. It helps you express to your drummer what sort of feel you're going for.

For example, if you want a really cheesy moment in a seventies-style soft rock love song, ask the drummer to brush some chimes slowly from side to side so they sound like they're tinkling in the distance.

If you want to give your song some *oomph*, ask your drummer to use the kick drum. It makes that deep "boom-boom" Tarzan sound.

Or let's say you want to zip up your number a bit, give it a bit of piz-zazz. Ask your drummer to stay on the snare drum. This should produce a "shuckha shickhe shuckha shickhe shuckha shickhe" sound, like your train's pulling in.

That's one of the great things about drummers: You can communicate with them by onomatopoeia. Just say, "I'd love a little 'boom-swoosh, boom-swoosh.'" Or, "Can you give me some 'taka-ticky, taka-ticky, taka-taka-toom' in this section?" Chances are, they'll get it.

Before we leave the drum kit, don't forget the hi-hat, the two smaller cymbals that a drummer moves together and apart with his foot pedal. And if you ever forget the name of it, just picture waving to someone, and saying, "Hiiiiiiiiiii! Haaaaaaaaat!"

I could go on and on about drums. We haven't even talked about the timpani yet. But I suspect you'd rather tell drummer jokes than learn the parts of a drum kit, so here's one more:

What do you call a guy who hangs out with musicians?
A drummer.

Don't Expect Much from Dating Services

ANY MUSICIAN WHO SPENDS a lot of time on the road learns not to expect much in the way of accommodations. I was easy to please by the time I made it to Boston, and a good thing, too. My Craigslist rental in Cambridge, Massachusetts, didn't look anything like its photos! I walked through the door and saw one light bulb dangling from the ceiling and several cockroaches scurrying across the floor. I was such a veteran tourer and so happy to be out of Toronto and on to a new adventure that I didn't mind, although I never brought food into that apartment again.

I signed up for classes at the Harvard Extension School summer program. First, a poetry class, then a class on postmodern literature, and then a class on German literature. I'd walk home along Massachusetts Avenue looking down at the red-brick sidewalks thinking what a different place I was in now. There was so much history there. Living in America was giving me a jolt.

Cambridge, across the Charles River from Boston, is its own universe, grittier than Toronto, and less self-conscious. Harvard Square is full of colourful people—everyone from buskers to homeless men playing chess on the sidewalks to the privileged Harvard students rushing off to class.

Oh all of the students rushing off to class
They are changing me and now I can't go back
Now I'm somewhere in between a pro and hack
                              ("World Away")

It was on one of my many walks to class on those sunny summer days in Cambridge that I picked up the scent of salt water coming off the ocean and suddenly felt my shoulders drop and my chin lift for the first time. My old Toronto posture, hunched and dragging my shoes along the sidewalk, melted away. Boston was a new beginning. I was happy for the first time in my adult life.

That autumn, I was accepted to Boston University. I began where I'd left off as an undergraduate twenty years earlier, taking classes in English and American Literature. I thrived in academia. They kept giving me As and A+s, which make you feel especially good. I made something called the dean's list two years in a row.

After a while, it became clear to me that academia is *so* different from the music business. In school, all you have to do is follow the rules and do what you're told and you will succeed. Not only that, they give you all kinds of accolades in school. I never got any prizes in music. Not even a pair of cheap plastic sunglasses. One day, I received a letter in the mail along with a pin to wear on my coat as a member of some Pi Delta Shmie Society. I accepted, even though I never made it to their Christmas dinners.

I was happy and new songs were flowing out of me. They were all about Boston and student life. I began to envision myself living there for good. The problem was I didn't know anyone. "You can't live in exile," somebody said to me. So I started to make an effort. I discovered a good way to meet people was by holding concerts in my living room. I invited the plumber, the mailman, the crossing guard, a few guys from the projects up the street, shopkeepers, several neighbours from the building, fellow dog walkers in the neighbourhood, some homeless people from Central Square.

By 2013, I had enough songs for my third album, *Gypsy Girl*. I recorded it between Toronto and Boston. I *had* to make the album. Even though my identity as a songwriter was falling away and I was taking a much-needed break from the music scene, it was a prolific time for me. My mind was opening up in academia and stimulating new material for songs. I had to get them in the studio.

Despite my house concerts, my loneliness persisted. I decided to try online dating as a way to meet people in Boston. I joined a site called OKCupid. Except after a while, I was calling it "OkStupid."

Do I need to explain why? Have you seen the profile pictures men put up on that site? Serial killers! One guy had a photo of himself walking around the side of his house dragging a heavy bag of garbage. Is that all Boston men have to do to rate as hot prospects? Take out the trash?

I met a few guys on OKStupid but they were nothing to write home about. One guy said he was a race-car driver, except it turned out he mostly raced his car was when I was in it. He used to text me pictures of himself in his race-car suit, with the helmet and everything, but he just looked more like an astronaut to me.

I once drove two hours to New Hampshire to watch him in a "race," except instead of crowds of people sitting in the bleachers there was only myself and my older lesbian friend Mary who came along for the ride. We stood behind a fence watching my OKStupid date speed around the race-track all by himself, several times until he started to get dizzy, I think. Or maybe it was Mary and me who were getting dizzy. Needless to say, that relationship went nowhere.

The next guy I met had studied drumming at Berkeley. He looked like a buff Jason Bateman and had some serious sex appeal. But he wore these long and pointy snakeskin boots that seemed a bit Mafia to me. They should have been a red flag. Every one of our dates ended with us up against my hallway wall, passionately kissing. And then I wouldn't hear from him for six weeks. We'd be out at a restaurant and a cute blond waitress would walk by and his eyes would be glued to her chest. That one didn't go anywhere, either.

Sometimes I'd look out my window on Magazine Street and watch the Harvard boys walk home from school in their preppy clothes, with their knapsacks on their back, wondering when romance was going to come for me. I wrote a song about it:

Oh you Harvard Boys
Playing your major chords
How do you find love

With that same sangfroid
Oh you Harvard Boys
Here in the neighbourhood.
        ("Harvard Boys")

Boston was lonely. But not long after my OKStupid failures, I met Dave.

Music Theory

YOU DIDN'T READ THAT HEADING and think this was going to be about music theory, did you? I don't know anything about music theory! Incidentally, that might explain why every song on my album *The Workingman's Blues* is in B-flat major. It's the only key I know.

Instead, I've always done everything by ear. I *tried* taking a theory class in my first year of university, and I failed. Not only that, my professor gave me an F. Do you know how many letter grades that is away from an A? Five! That's *five* letter grades away from an A! I would have got the message with a D-.

Does a songwriter have to know music theory to write songs? I say no. Irving Berlin couldn't read sheet music, and he did pretty well for himself. Are you familiar with "White Christmas?" Not too shabby.

Of course, it helps to know some basics. In my twenties, during one of my legendary depressive episodes, with nothing else to do with my life, I took guitar lessons and practised every day. I had a good teacher who went at my pace. "Just show me how to play 'When I Was a Boy' by Dar Williams," I said.

That meant *he* was the one who had to work out the mechanics of the song and show my fingers what to do on the guitar. I practised every day for hours. The only reason I'm a pretty good fingerpicker today is because of that depression. In six months, I learned enough technique to eventually develop my own style. So that's my prescription for you: a monumental depressive episode and six months of lessons on the instrument of your choice. (Just kidding. I wouldn't wish depression on anyone.)

My piano teacher in high school understood that I wasn't going to be able to read music so he figured out the Nina Simone and Elton John songs I liked and demonstrated, note for note, how to play them on piano. God bless the teachers out there who adapt to their students' special needs.

I'm always amazed when I go into the studio with super-talented session players. You'll play your song once and next thing they'll pull out a pencil and a piece of paper and start making charts. With any luck, your producer will also be a genius and translate what you've written to everyone else in that room. God bless those gifted and well-trained people who will take the burden off your hands.

Songwriting 101

L ET ME GUIDE YOU THROUGH the process of writing the title, verses, chorus, and a bridge for your first song, although you don't *have* to write a bridge if you don't want one. I mean, it's your song, right? I promise this will be a relaxed and easy experience.

Finding a title for your song is a good place to start. If you have a title, you have gold because it can inform what your song's going to be about from the get-go. You can even include the title somewhere in the chorus, for real impact. Take a deep breath in through your nostrils, then exhale slowly through your mouth (counting one Mississippi, and two Mississippi . . .) Repeat until you're totally at ease. Then pick up your pen and write a title. Any title. You can always change it later. Just get it down.

Still thinking about it? Don't panic. You're not going for Shakespeare. You're not going for *fancy*. Just write whatever comes to you.

Got it down? Good. And . . . relax.

After the title, the basic structure for a pop tune goes like this:

Verse
Verse
Chorus
Verse
Chorus
Bridge
Chorus

That doesn't mean you need to stick to the format. It is mere guidance. Again, you should write what you want. But let's say you do stick to the format.

The first verse is where you begin to tell the story in your song. You can start anywhere you want. Isn't that freeing? You could even begin by simply describing where you are. Or what you're doing at this moment. Or both: "Just a walk tonight / In the half moonlight / With my shoes scraping the ground."

Now you try. I'll wait.

Finished? Okay, now that you've written the first verse, you can begin to write the second verse, and then you're really on your way. Don't forget to breathe.

The second verse gets you into the meat of the story. This is where you need to delve a little deeper, expound on what you're trying to say, maybe develop a metaphor. And the reason I say "expound" is because it sounded good in my English papers.

Finished the second verse? Good. Now it's time for the chorus. This is where you really get to make a bang. The chorus is where you come to the point of what your song is about. It's kind of like the thesis, except you won't be graded. And try to make it pop! Try to make it catchy! You want this to be a moment for people to remember. You can even just repeat one word over and over for emphasis.

Isn't this exciting? Sitting here, I can feel your chorus bubbling up inside you. It's practically making my whole body shake! That, or the Dexedrine.

Got it down? Congratulations. You've almost completed your first song. Now add a final verse to wrap things up and bring closure to your story. And then you're done. Unless you want a bridge.

Having a bridge in a song is optional. You really don't need one but maybe there's just one other thing you really need to say in your song, something that will give it that little *je ne sais quoi*. The bridge is where you do it. It should also be a place where the melody changes.

It can be short. It can just be a couple of lines. Or you could just sing some "oohs" and "aahs." You could even let out a healthy scream. Why not? It would be cathartic. Whatever it does, your bridge should cross the song over into some other territory. That's why they call it a bridge.

I hope that's helped you sketch out your song. Now just rewrite it several hundred times until it practically sings itself.

Of course, you don't have to write songs in the manner I've suggested. You might want to come up with the chorus first, and then write the verses. You might write the title and then watch yet another episode of *Love It or List It*. That's fine.

There are no rules in songwriting. At least there aren't in Kat Goldman's Songwriting 101. Other coaches might tell you that this is the place where you use imagery. They might say, "Use rhymes," or, "Don't use rhymes." I say you should do what you want because it's your damn song. The only things I insist on are freedom and truth.

When I say freedom, I'm talking, let your freak flag fly. You can't write a song worrying what other people are going to think of it. You can't write a song by judging yourself. You want to enter a land without rules or inhibitions. Write the way hippies dance in a drum circle.

This is a bit of a tangent but in 1995, I went to the Rainbow Gathering in the New Mexico desert along with 30,000 other hippies. It was "fun," but I didn't catch a wink the whole time. All I could hear, all night long, was the sound of drum circles. Every single night it was the same god-damn thing: "Boom! Chucka-lucka-lucka. Boom! Chucka-lucka-lucka." Although, in fairness, it shifted every once in a while to: "Boom! Pum-pum-pum. Boom . . . pum!"

By the third day, although sleep deprived and starving because the Hare Krishna tent ran out of food, I finally started to get into the Rainbow vibe and decided to bathe in a beautiful, clear stream I'd discovered running down the mountain. I took off all my clothes, stretched my arms over my head, and delighted in the feeling of being naked as a baby, a true child of the earth, when all of a sudden I noticed Heimey Wasserman standing across the river from me, also naked.

"Hi," Heimey said, in his Long Island accent. "I'm Heimey. From Long Island." His chest was exceptionally hairy. There were even tufts of hair on his shoulders, and he had this large potbelly and a bushy beard. It dawned on me, as I floated on the surface of those crystalline waters, that my naked body had sparked the interest of Heimey from Long Island. I excused myself, grabbed my clothes, and headed back to my tent. But don't let that stop you from writing your song in a totally uninhibited manner. Play! Experiment! Let yourself go!

As for truth in your songs, why would you want anything less? The world is not very good truth anymore. Politicians lie to us. Advertisements lie to us. The shopkeeper at the clothing store told me I looked good in a light grey dress that I ended up buying. I got home, tried it on again, and saw that I looked like an elephant in a small tent. So fight back against lies by telling the truth in your songs.

(Another tangent. There are yoga centres and health facilities that offer self-help workshops where you can "share your truth" with a bunch of people you don't even know. Or you can go see a therapist and share your truth with her. The problem with therapists is that a lot of them don't give a rat's ass about you. The way you'll know this is if they start to doze off in front of you. I was once in the middle of some revealing monologue when I looked over and saw my therapist go limp in her arms. Next came the heavy eyelids, then her chin drooped to her chest, and her bottom lip parted slightly from the top. She was fast asleep in her chair for the remainder of our $200 session.)

My point is, who needs a self-help workshop or a narcoleptic therapist when you can share your truth with an audience through song?

Where Does a Song Come From?

WHERE DOES A SONG come from? How do you begin to answer a question that enigmatic? It's almost like asking, where does a baby come from? I mean, we know, of course, where a baby comes from (at least, I *think* I know), but we don't know why it happened in the first place. In other words, from where does life originate? Which reminds me of another question: Where do we go when we die? Is there an afterlife? Will there be hammocks?

Some songwriters have claimed their songs literally fly into their heads out of nowhere. Some dream their songs, or wake up with a melody in their head. How does that happen? Do elves whisper to them in their sleep? Are they making contact with other planets?

Can you pull out a song like a rabbit from a hat? How can it be that George Harrison wrote "While My Guitar Gently Weeps" by opening the pages of a book to the words "gently weeps?"

What about when a song gets written in fifteen minutes? How do you explain that? Does it just roll off your tongue into your fingers and onto your page? Does it write itself?

Is there really such a thing as a muse and, if so, can she *please* send me a hit for Stevie Nicks to cover?

How do you explain those long dry periods where you can't write a thing? You'll be thinking you're all washed up, you're ready to throw in the towel, your whole life has amounted to nothing, and you're ready to flip burgers at Dairy Queen. Then one day the spell breaks. Just like that, the wheels start turning and out comes another song.

Let's return to the original question. Where does a song come from? You might as well ask: Why is the sky blue? Why is water wet? Why did I get a little sister when I wanted a little brother? Why did Rachel Nussbaum punch me in the stomach at recess in grade four? If I drink ayahuasca tea, will I meet my True Self? And, finally, what is a True Self?

The answer is, I'm not sure. There are legitimate techniques for writing lyrics and melodies but some songs are simply inspired. You'll be driving home and see a billboard that gives you a first line, or a title. I get ideas when I'm scrubbing my bathroom floor. Maybe you'll be listening to your favourite music when a new melody gets sparked.

Songs come from a mysterious place. You just have to be there to catch them. And when those words come galloping through and you marry them to a melody, any songwriter knows it's one of the great feelings of being alive.

How Do You Find a Melody?

PEOPLE OFTEN ASK ME: Which comes first, the melody or the lyrics? The answer is: Neither, or either. Again, in Kat's classroom, there are no hard-and-fast rules. Take your melodies and words as they come.

Not too long ago, on one of those chilly November days in Toronto with the last brown leaves of autumn blowing in circles in the air, I was standing in the yard with my dog when these words came into my head: "The winds of change are blowin' in / The winds of change have come." And they were accompanied by a melody. Words and music, both at the same time. And it was a *beautiful* melody. "This is going to be big," I told myself. "This is going to be *off the charts*."

For the past year, the melody has kept flying around my head without landing anywhere. I haven't wanted to force it because the music feels special. Also, I haven't been able to finish the lyrics. I don't yet know what the song wants to say. But someday, I'm convinced, it will be huge.

Finding a melody is often the greatest challenge for the beginning songwriter. A melody is something ethereal. I don't think it's something you can force. It has to come from a feeling inside you. It should come from your heart and soul, and it should be intuitive.

I could say I'm going to teach you how to write a melody but I don't think melody is teachable. I believe that a melody has to come to you from your own imagination. I usually just hear melodies in my head. I'll wake up one morning and a melody will be there to greet me. It can happen anytime. At a bus stop or while you're brushing your dog's teeth. Whatever you're doing, be willing to receive it. Grasp it, write it down, never let it go. It just might be a hit.

The Beatles were some of the best melody makers I can think of but I also love Elton John, Simon and Garfunkel, Joni Mitchell, Jackson Browne, Carole King, James Taylor, Joan Armatrading, Cat Stevens—just about any of those great songwriters who came out of the sixties and seventies.

Christmas songs have some of the most beautiful melodies. My favourite is "O Holy Night." It's so moving, the way it lifts up at the end of the song. It gives me the shivers.

I guess my best tip would be to surround yourself with music that moves you. The more attention you pay to what other songwriters have done, the more adept you become at hearing and receiving melodies in your own head.

You could also pray for a melody. I do this for parking spaces and it often works.

Sometime after I heard my "Winds of Change" melody, I was at an all-inclusive resort in Mexico. I made the mistake of going by myself. Never do that. They make you feel so bad about it! You walk into the dining room and the hostess asks, "Just one person?"

"Yes," you say. And then your waiter comes over and asks the same question, "Just one person?"

"Yes. *Si*," you say, trying your Spanish.

"Only one?" he asks again.

"Uh-huh," you repeat. And then he makes a show of taking away the napkin, wineglass, and place setting of the person who is never going to be sitting in front of you. Then some woman from the resort comes over and gives you a questionnaire to fill out because obviously you have nothing better to do.

The worst is when you're sitting there at dinner and the mariachi band comes over to your table-for-one and starts playing "La Cucaracha." *Every single time* the trumpet player is flat, and there is nothing you can do about it.

Anyway, I was in the middle of my dinner-for-one, the mariachi band was finished, and they were playing Mexican pop music over the loud-speaker. Wouldn't you know it, a song came on that sounded exactly like my "Winds of Change"! I couldn't believe it! The *exact* same melody!

"Now what?" I said.

I had to think about it. Was anybody in Canada ever going to hear this Spanish song with the same melody as mine? It would probably never translate from one country to another. I was hoping that would get me off the hook.

The other thing I thought about was that some Mexican songwriter was on the exact same wavelength as me. Uncanny! Maybe we're kindred spirits. Maybe songwriters are connected on spectrums off limits to others. I take this to be a good thing.

I've decided I'm still going to write my "Winds of Change" song. And if one day I meet the Mexican songwriter who got hold of the melody before me, we will knock back a couple of tequilas, embrace each other, and run down the beach singing "La Cucaracha."

My Dream About Bob Dylan

I HAD A DREAM ABOUT BOB DYLAN. I was perched on the roof of some house. The shingles were made of black asphalt and the pitch of the roof was slight, not precarious. Bob Dylan appeared out of nowhere with a guitar in his hand. He was about to sing for the people below. He turned to me and said: "Can you please get off the rooftop, I have to play now." Clearly a rejection but I remembered he did say, "Please," so at least he was being polite about it.

That's it. That's all I remember. Ever since, I've been trying to make sense of the dream. I looked up the etymology of "rooftop" in Wikipedia. "Old English *hrof* ('roof; ceiling; top; summit; heaven; sky.')" Also, figuratively, the highest point of something.

And there was this, also on Wikipedia: "From Proto-Germanic *khrofam* (cf. Dutch roef 'deckhouse; cabin; coffin-lid.' Middle High German *rof* ('penthouse'). Old Norse *hrof* ('boat shed')."

I find it hard to pronounce words like "*khrofam*" and "*hrof*" but it's interesting that in these languages a roof is also considered the highest point of something, the sky, or heaven.

I wondered if it meant that Dylan had reached the highest point he could during his time in the music business.

I wondered if I was interloping by being on the rooftop, standing on his pitched turf? After all, there is no other Bob Dylan. Was it time for me to get off and stop trying?

Or maybe the dream spoke to me of reaching my own summit, of doing what I'm capable of doing in my own life.

Or maybe it summed up how I felt about the music business at that point. Maybe it was time to throw myself off the *hrof* and try something else. Like writing a book.

I would always be a songwriter. That was for certain. That would never change. But maybe it was time to stop chasing the dream of making it in a business that didn't bring enough reward.

That's not to say you shouldn't climb up on your own *khrofam*. But only do it because you love it. That's the only reason to be a songwriter, isn't it? That, and you never know who you'll meet up there.

You Will Meet a ~~Tall Dark~~ Stranger

ITH ALL YOUR TRAVELLING and performing, you're bound to meet new people and, if you're lucky, at least one of those people will be irresistible.

I first saw Dave moving heavy boxes down the hallway of my pre-war apartment building in Cambridgeport. He had this perfect nose: small, and straight, and it came to a little point at the end.

Next thing I knew, I was following him up the back of the moving ramp, where he was sitting on boxes with his work buddies, eating cheeseburgers. There was a tall guy with red hair who started flirting with me. He pronounced his *rrrr*'s as *ahhh*'s. I figured they were all from South Boston. A bunch of Southies. Red started to tell me they were all in a band. I figured he was showing off. All I wanted was to get to Dave.

I handed Red a copy of *Sing Your Song* to get rid of him and walked over to Dave and handed him my number on a scrap of paper.

"You should call me," I said. Part of my new Boston personality was to boldly ask guys out.

"Shuhhhh, Kat," Dave uttered between cheeseburger bites. He, too, had a South Boston accent. "I'll do that," he said.

Two days later the phone rang.

"It's Dave, from Wednesday."

Two months after that, he moved in. For the next three years, my life became a movie. *Good Will Hunting*. We were different people. Dave came from a working-class family on the South Shore. I came from a privileged family in Canada. At Easter and Christmas dinners at his folks' house, Dave's uncle, who belonged to some motorcycle gang, would sit across from me wearing a Harley Davidson T-shirt, looking at me like I was a Martian. He'd never come so close to a Jew.

"Would you like some honey ham?" his mother asked. "Oh, wait, do you eat ham?"

"Oh, no! I love ham, love it! Pile it on!" I said, chewing reluctantly on chunks of meat sweetened with pineapple and maraschino cherries.

One time, Dave came home with a sprained ankle. Said he'd been in a brawl with Red. Apparently they were fighting over me. I figured either Red had insulted me, or maybe he was jealous. The fight ended with Dave falling over and twisting his ankle.

"Wow! A fist fight?" my friend David Berman said at dinner in Toronto. "Cool."

I spent my days in classes or studying. Dave would get up at five and go to his blue-collar job. In the three years we lived together, he had a host of jobs, everything from moving furniture to sweeping chimneys to fixing coffee makers at Dunkin' Donuts. One Valentine's Day, he came home late from work with a pair of long-stemmed hot-pink roses in front of his soot-covered face. I'll never forget that image.

Some of our most romantic times were when we stayed at home during the "nor-eastuh" storms. I'd look out the living room into the garden and watch Dave playing with the dog in the snow. They'd play for hours. Dave would wave to me and smile with that hunky dimple in his cheek, all Ben Affleck.

Dave was also a fan and a great supporter of my music. When I returned from showcasing at the North East Folk Alliance conference, he gave me a *Star Wars* card that read: "The force must be very strong within you," and on the inside: "Congrats, my love, on a job well done. So proud of you, sweetheart." He was a very special guy. Dave was the kind of person who made you feel beautiful just because you were with him.

We even got engaged at one point. I took him to Nomad, my favourite hippie store in Cambridge, and chose a pretty gold ring for $400, with a tiny diamond in it. I paid for it myself, since Dave would never have been able to afford it. Afterwards, as we walked along Massachusetts Avenue, Dave knelt down on the sidewalk and proposed to me, making it official. We had all kinds of dreams, like moving to Baton Rouge, Louisiana, buying a little house, and opening a furniture consignment store. There were good times between us, until the morning of January 8, 2012, when the phone rang. It was my brother-in-law calling from Bancroft, Ontario.

"Kathy," he said, his voice going up at the end. "Bonnie died last night."

I stood in my hallway, my face buried in Dave's beefy shoulders, and cried. My older sister was dead at forty-seven.

Dave said I was never the same after my sister died. He would come home cranky from work, not having had any lunch money. I'd be curled up on the sofa, too depressed to make dinner. We'd fight over stupid things, like why I used a fork instead of a spoon to stir my coffee. Why I wasted my accident money on buying more furniture for the apartment. Why I'd keep making him move the furniture around to suit my latest decorating whim.

Our fights ended with him snapping open large green garbage bags, throwing all his belongings inside, slamming my front door, and screeching off in his car, back to Hanover to stay with his parents. Dave would get a furrowed brow when we fought, and have a mean look on his face again. The neighbours could hear our screaming matches. Before long, he was disappearing on weekends to the Cape to hang out with his younger friends, or staying up all night in his father's garage to work on his car. Another woman came into his life.

In the summer of 2014, my front door slammed for the last time and Dave left for good. After that, I found myself living with ghosts in the apartment. I managed to finish my degree at Boston University and I was getting ready to start grad school but Boston was never the same. I couldn't regain my Cambridge footing.

Grad school had seemed like the right thing. Straight from my bachelor's degree, I enrolled to do a master's in expressive arts therapies at Lesley University in Cambridge. I figured it was time to find a real profession, something altruistic, something less self-indulgent than being an artist, something that produced tangible results, and something that would pay the bills.

What is expressive arts therapy? Wikipedia says:

> *Expressive arts therapy is the practice of using imagery, storytelling, dance, music, drama, poetry, movement, horticulture, dreamwork, and visual arts together, in an integrated way, to foster human growth, development, and healing.*

In the autumn of 2005, I drove two hours from Boston to a retreat centre in Maine where students came together for a week-long orientation. I parked my car in the parking lot and found the dining hall where we signed in, picked up our orientation binders, and stuck name tags on our shirts. After lunch, all three hundred expressive arts therapies students gathered in a circle in a large field.

"Welcome to first-year orientation!" a staff member shouted. And then it happened. One of the professors stood in the middle of the circle with a conga drum and started to bang it.

"BOOM! Chucka-lucka-lucka, BOOM! Chucka-lucka-lucka."

"Oh god!" I said to myself. "Not the conga drum!"

Somewhere in the middle of the "boom chucka-lucka-luckas," they asked us to go around the circle and say our names. When it came close to my turn, I snuck out of the circle and bushwhacked my way through the forest to the parking lot, where I lit up a cigarette in my car to think.

If I stayed, it meant three years of conga drums. I wasn't up for that. But if I left the program, I'd lose my student visa. I'd have no choice but to say goodbye to Boston, pack everything up, and move back to Toronto. Sometimes life turns on a dime. Sometimes you are moved by passions you can't explain. I drove back to Boston, listening to the Indigo Girls the whole way home, dropped out of graduate school the next day, and, after seven years in the United States, returned to Toronto.

What Women Get
Called in Music

WHAT IS IT WITH some guys in this business? Do they think playing an instrument gives them a free pass to be jerks to women?

Folk musicians, especially. What makes them think they're so cool? They get up there, flipping their hair, fingerpicking their banjos really fast, singing "Puff the Magic Dragon" in three-part harmony, trying to show off to the girls but come on! Get a grip! You're a folk musician! You're not *that* cool!

And why do some guys in this business think they can get away with calling women "babe" or "darlin'" or "sweetie," when, really, you just met them five minutes ago? Oh. And I've never understood this one: "Chick." Why do some guys in music have to call you "chick?" Does it look like I have soft yellow feathers and webbed feet? Does it look like I waddle when I walk? Don't answer that.

What I'm trying to say is that it hasn't been easy working as a woman in the music industry. Often, you're the only female in the room. People will take advantage of you.

Take, for example, the two blockheads I called my band in the early 2000s. A rookie drummer and a degenerate bass player, neither of whom showered. I brought them to my cottage one summer to record an album.

The bass player and I got into it one day. I called him on not washing the fry pan after he'd cooked a cheeseburger for himself. This incensed him. Next thing I knew, both of them were driving off in the rental car that I'd paid for, all the way back to Toronto. And they made off with the recordings that legally belonged to me. After that, I had to sneak over to the bass player's house, dressed like the Unabomber, wearing dark sunglasses and a hoodie, to slip a lawyer's letter into his mailbox demanding the return of my recordings. I never got them back. I call it my lost album.

You have to be so careful who you play with in this business! Always hire musicians who are kind and respectful.

And how about—and I really love this one—when they call women divas or prima donnas when you are simply asking for what you need to get your work done. Did it ever occur to them that you know what you're talking about? I once had a producer accuse me of being a diva for doing forty-five vocal takes on a song. Turns out he was exaggerating. Most times, the tape stopped rolling after just a few seconds when my voice kicked out. And so *what* if it took forty-five times for me to sing the track? It's *my* voice on the album! I want it to sound good! And who do you think is paying the bills for the whole thing?

I mentioned this in a social media post a few years back. I explained how women often get called prima donnas when they ask for what they need in music. "Spoken like a true prima donna," a former guitar player of mine commented. This after I'd paid him top dollar to work on my album. What an asshole.

Here's another one. The guitar player who complained at the end of the night that he didn't get enough money, even though I made $80 and gave him $100. Another asshole.

I'm telling you, I've come across some real lowlifes. This is why I have so much respect for Heart. Now there were two chicks who really held their own. Talk about kick-ass. I bet they didn't take crap from band members. Would *you* mess with two women who can rock it out like that, to "Baracuda"?

A Good Producer

I T'S TAKEN YOU YEARS to write your songs and now it's time to record them. You're beyond excited because this is the moment to finally catalogue your new material. It's time to find a good producer. Here are some tips.

First of all, make sure you don't hire someone who on your first day of recording answers the door in a cloud of marijuana smoke.

Be prepared to fire anyone who brings back beers and babes to the recording studio. There's nothing worse than singing a meaningful ballad in the vocal booth and looking out to see your producer with a blonde in his lap. On *your* dime.

The worst is having a producer who thinks he knows everything and makes you feel like you know nothing. Don't work with a producer who leaves you out of the process or tries to intimidate you with Kim Jong-Un lines like: "Knowledge is power!" Fascist dictators are totally out.

Your producer should treat you as his equal. You should feel he is on your side. He should be holding your hand along this sacred journey. You should see him as your midwife. Better yet, your shaman, wearing a white loincloth and blowing into a conch shell, breathing life into your songs.

Most likely, your producer will be proficient on his computer, clicking like a pro. That proficiency makes the process go swiftly and you're paying the bills.

With luck, he or she will also encourage your best performance and know how to create a comfortable atmosphere. You want to feel like you can kill it in the studio. You want to laugh and have fun. That's what making music should feel like, right? It should make you want to shimmy, and shout, and shake it all about, and do the hokey-pokey and turn yourself around. You don't want to be crying with frustration and running to entertainment lawyers to rewrite your $250-an-hour recording contract.

Most of all, a good producer should be someone you can trust. A good producer will never pressure you to share the rights to one of your songs, just because he added a couple of lines of music. That would just be pushy, unfair, and dishonest, wouldn't it? In fact, only a crook will try to steal your song out from under you, especially if you've presented the song in its entirety, with lyrics and melody complete, before entering the studio.

When your producer plays back your final tracks, it should bring tears to your eyes. Good tears. You won't believe where he has taken your songs. The experience

will forever change you. You'll think of your producer as Moses coming down the mountain with his long white hair, with the holy tablets in a CD case. And you will always be grateful, because a new album is one of the greatest gifts of your life.

You Might Try Volunteering

I F YOU STAY IN THE music business long enough and, like me, fail to earn enough money to support yourself, someone is likely to suggest that you volunteer your time to a good cause. Because isn't that what you're doing as a musician, anyway?

When I returned home to Toronto from Boston, my mother kept saying: "Volunteer! That's where you're gonna meet somebody!"

But I'd tried volunteering and it never worked for me. I'd go to the first meeting but then get so anxious and depressed, I'd never make it back for the second. That, or the volunteer coordinator would yell at me for something.

One time I volunteered as an art therapist for a high school class of troubled teenagers. I showed up ten minutes late. The teacher gave me hell about it. She took me aside in the staff room and really gave me what for. You would have thought I'd killed a member of her family. I felt terrible about it. At the same time, who was she to yell at me? I was an unpaid volunteer.

Another time, when I was in college, I volunteered at a Jewish centre for older adults in Worcester, Massachusetts. I put my all into that one. I sketched out plans for what I was going to do in the group. Devised workshops. One day, I brought in a ghetto blaster, played some soca music, and got all the seniors in a conga line, kicking their legs out from side to side, holding the shoulders of the person in front of them as they moved around in a circle.

They loved it. Everyone was really into it but the volunteer coordinator was outraged. She was shooting me dirty looks from across the room. You would have thought I'd brought them pot to smoke! I guess the conga wasn't in her comfort zone.

Having been yelled at for not doing enough at one position, and receiving the evil eye for outdoing myself at another, I thought I was done with volunteering but I decided to take my mother's advice and try again. I offered my services to a seniors' centre near my new apartment in midtown. I thought I could offer a creative writing class, maybe teach songwriting, or at least do something creative. Somehow the volunteer coordinator didn't catch wind of this. She assigned me to lead a current events group for senior women.

Except I don't know anything about current events! And right in the middle of the session, one of the senior women started yelling at me: "What do you know about current events?"

This started a war with the other women in the group: "It's not her fault!" one of them said.

Yeah, it wasn't my fault! And whose lousy idea was it to have me lead a current events group? I'm a songwriter, for crying out loud! Thank god for the cookie plate. It was lying right there in front of me. As the women shouted at one another across the large boardroom table, I cleared the plate of oatmeal cookies.

I guess I don't have to tell you that I never made it back for the second session. Instead, I spent the next two years in my apartment, wearing the red fuzzy robe, writing and rehearsing songs for my fourth album, *The Workingman's Blues*.

Masterpieces

AT SOME POINT IN your career, you will do your very best work. It may come early, it may come late, but it will come.

Mine came late. When I was back in Toronto, *The Workingman's Blues* became an obsession for me. You would have thought I was trying to paint the ceiling of the Sistine Chapel. I'm not sure what was driving me so hard with that album. Maybe I had unresolved issues from the breakup with Dave. Maybe I was desperately trying to figure out where I belonged between Boston and Toronto. For some reason, I felt this had to be a defining album for me. It had to be the best work I'd ever done in music.

I wrote a lot of bad songs to get to the good ones. The best came just days before I went into the studio in one last push. "Take It Down the Line" and "Baby, I Understand" were pivotal numbers that gave the record its ultimate purpose, finding compassion for the workingman of America, and saying goodbye to my own American Dream.

Except for mandatory walks with the dog, I didn't leave the apartment. The red fuzzy robe never came off. My friends began to get the picture. If they wanted to see me, they had to come to my place. I work shopped many of the songs in rehearsals with some wonderful musicians in Toronto. I did house concerts and shows to practise. Several times I went into studios to record, only to realize I wasn't ready yet. I started the album five times before it finally came together with producer Bill Bell.

On its release, Stevie Connor from www.bluesandrootsradio.com wrote: "'The Workingman's Blues' is a masterpiece of our generation." No money changed hands. It was named one of the top albums of 2017 by the Australian publication *Timber and Steel*. I got play on folk radio stations and the Stingray channel. The best was my release at Hugh's Room, where we ended the night with "Release Me." I had the three women in hot-pink dresses from the video dancing onstage beside me. Man. Did they ever give it.

And then, on cue, the day after my release, I crashed. I crashed so hard I couldn't move off my sofa for months. I felt lost and without purpose all over again. I was inconsolable. Until one day, Stevie Connor wrote me from out of the blue and said: "Kat, how'd you like to write a blog for our website about your experiences as a songwriter?"

Well, that was it. The blog was called *The Disgruntled Songwriter*, and people didn't hate it. Soon I was turning out chapters for a book. That's how this whole thing got started.

Post-Album Blues

I T WAS THE MIDDLE OF WINTER with sub-zero temperatures in Toronto and I was in a slump. I had just released an album and, after riding a three-year crest of writing, recording, and promotion, I came crashing down into a great black hole.

Every time I went to order a coffee at Starbucks, I would break down sobbing, and not just because I couldn't pronounce "Grande Caramel Macchiato." I wore my pajamas and day clothes interchangeably for months. Even the dog seemed down. I was suffering from a bad case of the post-album blues.

Thing is, once you release your album, you have no idea how to get people to hear it. You go from being a creator to a gladiator, fighting to have your album recognized in a market saturated with songwriters. You hope, with all your might, for success. You work for success with everything you've got. But the reality is that after six months, people lose interest in your project.

With every new album, you hope all over again. This is the one. This is the album, honed by your craft and vision, that will be recognized by hordes of people, mostly in America. You begin to fantasize that Emmylou Harris will call and ask you to tea, and will cover one of your songs. Elton John will invite you to one of his wild, lavish parties, and let you sit on his piano and try on his sunglasses. You will sit around Big Pink with Bob Dylan and Robbie Robertson, eating barbecue, trading off songs on guitar around a campfire.

After all the hard work that goes into it, and the extraordinary high you get from working with a great producer and supremely talented musicians—after spending each day in the studio with a strong and unique sense of purpose—everything comes to a grinding halt and you are veritably lost. Burned out. Just plain spent.

I decided it was time to go to Mexico. I needed to speak to Arturo, a psychic in Playa del Carmen.

For forty American dollars, Arturo will read your tarot cards. He's a gifted telepath who grew up near the Texas border. He looks partly like a wizard, partly like Jesus, with long, straggly blond hair and piercing blue eyes (that's Jesus, right?). I found him in the same spot where I last saw him, five years earlier, at the same table, drinking a fruit smoothie, three blocks from the beach.

I asked Arturo my biggest question: "Where is my music career heading?" No surprise, I drew the Death card. But Arturo said it signified good changes ahead.

"You're going to have people helping you," he said.

"Really?" I asked. "People are going to help me?"

"Yes, in the next year. You are going to be rewarded for your efforts. Just keep going."

"Wow," I said, exhaling. "So just keep at it then?"

"Just keep at it."

"You don't think I should go into law or something? There's still time for a master's degree. Or what about doing a chair yoga Program, you know, where you teach yoga from a chair? How hard could it be? All you have to do is sit there . . . in a chair!"

"You are on the *right* path," Arturo said. "Don't worry. People are going to help you. Now. Let's talk about your hair."

"My hair?"

"You need to change your hair."

"Really?" I said, tilting my head to one side. "That's funny, because I had actually been wondering lately whether to grow it long or keep it short."

"Shorter would be better," he said in his sexy Spanish accent.

"Interesting. So you think shorter, then?"

"Yes."

"And bangs? What do you think of bangs?"

"You could do bangs."

I was so relieved. His clairvoyance was off the charts.

That night I walked along the beach and looked up at the vast spread of stars in the Mexican sky. I could hear a melody forming in my head. It was a new song that wanted to be written. I knew in that moment I had to keep going. Success or not, I realized I could never stop making music.

I always find the answers in Mexico. *Olé!*

The Long Haul

YOU WILL BE ASKED if you're going to be in the music business for the long haul. You'll be asked if you've written any songs lately. If you answer, "Not really," people will question whether you'll ever write songs again, or whether you're a songwriter for real.

One time I overheard a bunch of session players. "He's a lifer," one of them said, meaning this person would always work in the music business, that he'd never give up, that he had what it took—commitment!—to keep his songs coming.

I never like it when I hear people talk about who's a lifer and who isn't, because it implies judgment. And who really knows if your songs are going to keep coming? You might not write any for a couple of years and then one day a bunch will come spewing out. Sometimes songwriters have to do some living first, before they can produce new material.

Years ago, I bumped into an old high school friend at the gym. "I've met a guy," she told me, "and we're in it for the long haul."

It really bugged me. What did she know about long hauls? How can you be certain what will happen in your life? Tomorrow you could be crushed by a car inside a bagel store!

Anyway, I've never had a relationship that was for the long haul. Although I've had boyfriends who might have felt they were hauling me along, and vice versa.

Just because you're not writing songs or performing doesn't mean you're not in it for the long haul. I figure if you've written one good song, you're a songwriter and you'll always be one. It's in you. The door will always be open for more songs to come.

Just because you're not getting a record deal, or selling lots of albums, or touring frequently, does not make you any less of a songwriter. Don't pay attention to other people's expectations and deadlines. That's one advantage of being an indie artist: you don't have a record company breathing down your neck, pressuring you to make a new album. Take your time, honour your rhythm. When your songs are meant to come, they will.

What's So Great About a Rock Star?

I WAS HAVING DINNER with my family at a Middle Eastern restaurant in Toronto when I noticed a rock star sitting at the next table next to us. His hair was a classic 1970s mullet (much better than my mullet), and he was wearing vintage eyeglasses, blue jeans, and a denim jacket. I was giddy.

As you can imagine, I'd been waiting for this moment since I'd missed my chances with Phil Collins and Tony Bennett. I started to fidget through my purse for a copy of my CD. (Always bring a CD in your purse!) Thank goodness I had one this time. I took a few deep breaths and then ever so nonchalantly tiptoed to his table where he was sitting with his girlfriend and a group of hipster-looking friends.

"Hi," I said. "I'm a big fan of your music. I'm also a songwriter and I was wondering if I could give you a copy of my new album." I carefully pulled out my CD *The Workingman's Blues* and presented it to him face up, with the picture of me in the Cher wig on the cover. "It's a rock musical," I told him, "and the songs tell a story about a young workingman from Boston who's had a troubled past."

The rock star was cordial. Friendly, even. He accepted my gift graciously, despite dirty looks from his girlfriend. I thanked him. I must have been really nervous, because I formed my hands into a prayer sign in front of my chest and started to make small bows to him as I gently backed away from his table. I next bolted for the exit, tripping on the carpet on my way out, and lit up a cigarette on the sidewalk.

I started to review the scene in my mind. How was my pitch? Too long? Under one minute, I think. Was I smooth? How did I look? I caught a reflection of myself in the window. Goddamn it. I'm twenty-five pounds overweight and it's all gone to my stomach! Why the hell did I wear these baggy cut-off jeans today? This is the worst outfit I've ever worn! I look like a rhino in pedal-pushers!

Then I shifted to the old familiar narrative. What if he listens to my CD and likes it? Or, what if he throws it in a garbage bin as he leaves the restaurant? I realized it's between those extremes that I've lived my life as a songwriter.

I took the long way back to my table to keep a low profile. "What's so great about a rock star?" my mother asked. It was a good question, and I thought about it the whole way home in the back seat of my parents' station wagon.

That was my mother's question, and it was apt. What *is* so great about rock stars? They're regular, everyday people. What makes them special? Why do they get to strut around acting like gods in black leather pants and black leather jackets with their perfect hair blowing in the wind?

And what is it with the hair, anyway? Obviously, it's a crucial aspect of their look. I mean, can you imagine a bald rock star? Just try to picture Mick Jagger with a shaved head. Just try to imagine Twisted Sister in pixie cuts. It would never work out. I bet it takes a lot of product to make their hair look so good. Either that or they never wash it.

Which reminds me: Why are rock stars always so dirty? Sure, until they make it, they're loading and unloading equipment, sleeping on buses, crashing on sofas, rolling in beer-soaked sheets in cheap hotels. But once they've made it, why are they still booking accommodation without showers? Or soap.

And why is it that rock stars always get special treatment? The time I was standing in the customs line at Logan airport, one of the guards recognized Phil Collins and let him through to the first available agent, ahead of the rest of us. Even Phil seemed embarrassed by it. This is what I'm trying to say. Rock stars are always getting coddled. And you wonder why they never act like grown-ups.

We put them on such a pedestal. We give them so much power. All those screaming girls when the Beatles first played Shea Stadium—overkill! I can't understand why women throw themselves at rock stars. Have they never heard of sexually transmitted diseases? I know a famous musician from London who said his bandmates used to have sex with two women at a time. I don't get it. Why do they need more than one? It's so greedy. Rock stars think they can get away with anything.

What annoys me most is that rock stars have such confidence. Look at Steven Tyler. The guy oozes self-esteem. What gives him such conviction? Just because he's thin, has a cool goatee, and can do a high leg kick doesn't mean he's the best thing since ice cream. Get over yourself! I can kick my leg as high as you! The only difference is you can bring yours back down again.

I know I'm giving rock stars a bad rap but I'm sure they're not all ego-maniacal. It could be I've caught them on bad days. Or maybe they're just out of sorts from travelling so much. Imagine all those hours sitting on a plane, crunching your vertebrae, or trying to sleep on a bus where every-one's up all night playing Xbox. Touring at that level has to be hard work. And staying up for long hours, partying with chicks, having to be *on* all the time. Imagine having to scream "We're gonna *rock* you tonight!" in front of 60,000 people when you just want to be home in your jammies, watching *Mad Men*.

I bet that some of those big shots are actually very shy and sensitive people. For all we know, they spend their spare time watching chick flicks starring Meg Ryan.

Or maybe it's like they say: they've "paid their dues," and don't have to care anymore about how they behave.

The more I think about it, the more I have to admit we owe a lot to rock stars. After all, they inspire us. We delight in their talent. Their songs bring meaning to our lives. Where would be now without "Bridge Over Troubled Water," "My Way," "Halleluja," "We Built This City?"

Would we ever be able to unleash our wild and free spirits without rock stars to show us the way? Whenever I watch videos of Elvis singing "Polk

Salad Annie" in his white Vegas suit, it makes me want to unleash my own wildness. Something about the way he gyrates, thrusting his hips out when he sings the "Polk" part. I love it when he winds his arm in the air, like he's getting us ready for something special. "Polk! Polk salad!" And then, when he starts to shimmy, it makes *me* want to shimmy. It's electrifying. I'm telling you, Elvis really knew how to do it. Looks to me like his backup singers were also getting revved up when Elvis sang the "Polk!" part. I bet they wouldn't have minded, and I wouldn't have either, if Elvis had given them a little "Polk!" in their "salad."

How Do You Know
When You've Made It?

T HAT'S PROBABLY ENOUGH about rock stars but I have to mention one other problem they create. They upstage people who have less talent. Think how that makes us look. Okay, so maybe we don't sing as well, or can't write hit songs, but do you have to flaunt it, take up all the oxygen in the room? How do you think it makes us feel?

There's nothing like a rock star to make us poor independent songwriters feel like schlumps. They set impossible standards, which is why it's so important to define success on your own terms. Don't set the bar too high, is what I'm trying to say. Rejoice in hearing your song on a local radio station for the first time. Or in making your first $10 at a gig.

Here are some of the times I felt like I'd made it.

I was at my local natural food store, run by a very sweet Korean couple, and just as I was paying for my oil of oregano, I heard a song from my album *The Workingman's Blues* playing over the loudspeaker. Incredible, I thought, until I remembered I'd given them a copy the year before. But still, it was me. And maybe someone buying calendula cream would also hear it. Remember, you're going for one fan at a time.

Another glorious moment was when I was flipping through a jukebox machine in a tiny bar on Dundas Street West, and found a copy of my first CD in the racks. Astounding, I thought. My music's in a jukebox. How did it get there? I had no idea. But it was *there* and I was not hallucinating.

I went home that night with a huge smile on my face, rejoicing at the idea that I had attained local notoriety in Toronto.

Hearing one of my songs on CBC Radio for the first time was also a thrill. And it's always a gas when my savvy, twenty-three-year-old nephew quotes from my songs.

It was an honour receiving my first recording grant from a legitimate arts council. It made me feel like I'd finally been recognized as a true artist—by my own government, no less!

But probably my greatest high was opening for Al Stewart at the Bottom Line in New York City. A voice came over the loudspeaker during sound check: "Kat, what colour lights would you like on you tonight?" Coloured lights? I'd never been asked that before. That was when I knew I'd made it to the big time. I had to think on my feet. Let's see, green would be bad for the pallor and yellow, too, would be sickly.

"Anything in the red or blue family!" I blurted out, feeling proud of myself.

That night I wore a pair of rolled-up jeans, hot-pink pumps, and my hair was done in curls. I had a band supporting me. We'd had a couple of rehearsals that week in the city. Well, not only did we not suck, the crowd went wild. Some guy kept yelling "Bravo!" after I played "Music Teacher." And right before I got off the stage, someone in the front row handed me a note that said: "Year of the Kat," a play on the Al Stewart hit.

It meant I was *in*, and it felt good. When I got backstage, Al shook my hand and congratulated me on a great set. The band complained about not getting paid enough as my manager whisked me into my dressing room where I celebrated with friends from New York and Toronto. It was one of those great nights that remind us why we do it.

The independent songwriter has to define her own success. We're in a business where it seems no matter how hard you work or how talented you are, you can never catch a break. But maybe, at the end of the day, success is as easy as hearing someone say, "You are good. You exist. Your work means something." To have that one person tell you that your music reminded them of someone they lost, or that you articulated something they couldn't have themselves, can make it all worthwhile. That's when you can say, "I was here. My songs mattered. I wasn't a schlump after all."

Advice to Your Younger Self

MY ADVICE TO MY YOUNGER SELF who is thinking of making a career in the music business is simple: Get out! Get out now and never look back. That is no place for a nice young woman like yourself to spend the best (and most fertile) years of your life. Find a good man. Settle down. Have a few babies, take some extra time off for maternity leave.

Or don't find a man. Who needs one? The only thing good that came out of one of my relationships was someone to loofah my back in the shower every once in a while.

Get a law degree. Train in chair yoga. Become a building inspector, a house flipper, a reiki master, a candystriper, a CEO of your own made-up company, open a furniture consignment store, import Moroccan pillows, rescue stray dogs in Mexico, sell fake Fendi purses downtown. Hot dog stand?

Do what you want. Just don't waste your time slogging it out in the music business. Even if you'll love it like I did. Even if—admit it, dammit!—you'd do it all over again.

Songwriters I'm Dying to Meet

THERE ARE SO MANY SONGWRITERS who've touched my life and influenced my own music but there are three in particular I'm dying to meet. Paul McCartney, Shawn Colvin, and Bob Dylan.

I've often imagined how these meetings will go. When I meet Paul McCartney, I will start to cry. Paul will wrap his arms around me, give me a warm hug, and say in his lovely accent: "Oh, now, no need for tears, then!"

We'll be on a comfy couch with tea and scones and heavy cream and I'll ask how he wrote "Maybe I'm Amazed" and tell him how its melody always touches me. He'll hold my hand as we skip through a rose garden and I'll go on and on about his perfect melodies, and how I can only aspire to write melodies that perfect one day.

I'll tell Paul that "Let It Be" makes me feel close to god or something, and that I work out to *Ram* on my stationary bike. Our mullets will blow in the wind as we ride through London on the top level of a double-decker bus, laughing and waving to the people in the street below. As we walk around Piccadilly Circus, I'll tell Paul how sorry I am about John, and George, and, of course, Linda. In Madame Tussauds, I will touch his shirt and stick my nose into it to smell it. It will have a fresh and cozy scent. Then I'll pinch his apple cheeks, making them even rosier. Before we part, I'll ask if I can visit again sometime, and Paul will say, "Of course! Anytime!"

My meeting with Bob Dylan will be different. Bob will come over to my apartment where we'll sit and get down to business. We'll look into each other's eyes and there will be an instant connection. I'll feed him, and for once I won't be a terrible cook. I'll make him my mother's brisket, because it's sweet and juicy and goes well with challah.

I'll tell him about my bagel store and he'll sit there listening quietly.

Eventually Bob will start talking in epigrams, like in his biography. "You have to learn how to hoard your energy."

I'll ask him what he thinks of death, and god, and the afterlife. He'll sit back and give me the gems of wisdom he's acquired over the years. "A man is a success if he gets up in the morning and goes to bed at night and in between does what he wants to do." All the while we'll be looking into each other's eyes.

I'll play him my hit song "Annabel" over my Bose speakers and tell him that he inspired it. Bob will get the song right away and smile. Then I'll tell him there are a bunch of very disheveled people on YouTube who cover it and he'll know exactly what I mean. I'll play "Baby, I Understand" and tell him it won "finalist" in a songwriting competition in Nashville, even though they never gave me any prizes. Bob will like the song so much, he'll play it for Emmylou Harris, who will cover it on her next album and make it a worldwide smash.

After that, Bobbie and I will sing "Boots of Spanish Leather," exchanging verses back and forth, still looking into each other's eyes. At the end, we'll shake hands, still looking into each other's eyes, and I will never see him again. But I will have a new confidence in my skills and become prolific and write seven more albums.

When I meet Shawn Colvin, and this will really happen, we'll go shopping in thrift stores and try on different outfits and share lots of giggles. "You should try this one!" Shawn will say, holding up a funky dress, and it will fit me perfectly and she'll buy it for me. Then we'll go to a greasy spoon, have some eggs and toast, and talk about music, life, and men, drink gallons of coffee, and maybe shed a few tears. Feeling kinda high, we'll go back to my apartment and really get high. I'll play her first CD, *Steady On*, over my Bose speakers and skip to the third track, "Shotgun Down the Avalanche," and say, "Shawn, this song changed my life."

Then I'll put on her song "New Thing Now" and tell her how I drove twelve hours from Boston to Toronto listening to it on repeat. When it's time to say goodbye, I'll form my hands into a prayer position in front of my chest, say "Namaste" (something I learned at the ashram, meaning, "I honour the god in you"), make a little bow to her, and add, "Shawn, it was because of you I became a songwriter."

Afterword

STILL HOLD ON TO the bucket list I made after my accident, and I've crossed off a few items from it. I've made four albums, earned a degree. I'm writing this book. I've had the pleasure of raising my amazing dog Max, and watching my beautiful niece and four nephews blossom into wonderful people. I've met all kinds of interesting people along the way: songwriters, musicians, rock stars, academics, poets, actors, dancers, yogis, therapists, rabbis, shamans, circus people, magicians, workingmen, crossing guards, and even some of the guys from the projects in Cambridge. I've started teaching songwriting to individuals in Toronto and sometimes I teach art for kids. I haven't ruled out the chair yoga instructor program.

It's funny, this past week I've had a melody gnawing at my brain, screaming at me to write it. Day and night, I can't get it out of my head. I think I'll eventually succumb. And, who knows, maybe it will be a keeper.

How can I stop? Writing songs is like breathing for me. I suspect I'll always be doing it. I'm pretty sure it was my destiny to write songs. It's who I am, even if I never sell any albums. And even if those crass, egomaniacal music executives never return my emails, I'll probably just keep making songs right up until the end. I guess that means I'm a lifer.

Acknowledgements

THANK YOU TO THE FOLLOWING for their enormous support and encouragement: Bernie and Fran Goldman, Artie Martello, Ellie Tesher, Viane Ewart, Stephen Tesher, Jonas Goldman, Lorne Marin, Johnny Epstein, Brock Simpson, Evan Ritchie, Linda Saslove, Michael McKenzie, Cynthia French, Glen Hornblast, the late James McCallum, Ruth Hazelton, Bill Bell, Julie Tator, Daniel Miller, John Miller, Anne Connor, Jeff Stone, Alex Wong, Megan Slankard, Douglas September, Ruth Schweitzer, Sarah Greene, Bruce Alpert, Arlis Barclay, Michael Laderoute, Arlo Burgon, Dar Williams, Paul Fraser, Shawn Colvin, Matthew Bucemi, Nina Berkson, and Rebecca Eckler.

My special thanks to Stevie Connor for asking me to write a blog for his website, and to Ken Whyte, at Sutherland House Books, for his belief in me.